W9-BUR-202

ACCOUNTING

Professional Careers Series

 in

ACCOUNTING

GLORIA L. GAYLORD,
GLENDA E. RIED

FOURTH EDITION

McGraw·Hill

New York   Chicago   San Francisco   Lisbon   London   Madrid   Mexico City
Milan   New Delhi   San Juan   Seoul   Singapore   Sydney   Toronto

Library of Congress Cataloging-in-Publication Data

Gaylord, Gloria L.
     Careers in accounting / by Gloria L. Gaylord, Glenda E. Ried.—4th ed.
          p.   cm. — (McGraw-Hill professional careers series)
    Includes bibliographical references.
    ISBN 0-07-145873-5 (alk. paper)
     1. Accounting—Vocational guidance—United States.   2. Accounting—Vocational
guidance—Canada.   I. Ried, Glenda E.   II. Title.

HF5616.U5G39   2006
   657'.023'73—dc22
                                   2005022623

1 2 3 4 5 6 7 8 9 0   DOC/DOC   0 9 8 7 6

ISBN 0-07-145873-5

McGraw-Hill books are available at special quantity discounts to use as premiums and sales
promotions, or for use in corporate training programs. For more information, please write to the
Director of Special Sales, Professional Publishing, McGraw-Hill, Two Penn Plaza, New York, NY
10121-2298. Or contact your local bookstore.

This book is printed on acid-free paper.

CONTENTS

CHAPTER 11
Maximizing Your Career   163
Being organized · Communicating · Maintaining a
career-oriented attitude · Being assertive · Using power ·
Finding a mentor · Networking · Promoting yourself · Notes ·
Suggested reading

APPENDIX A
National Accounting-Related Organizations   175

APPENDIX B
Major Accounting Journals of
Academic and Professional Societies   179

APPENDIX C
State Boards of
Accountancy in the United States   181

APPENDIX D
Canadian Resources   187

FOREWORD

Just reading the financial section of any newspaper will tell you that today's business world is more complex than ever. Financing arrangements are more sophisticated, tax and accounting regulations are more complicated, and borrowing and investing tactics that were unheard of a few years ago are now commonplace. As a result, Certified Public Accountants are in greater demand than ever. CPAs help individuals and businesses sort through the maze and plan strategies for a successful future. The financial information that professional accountants provide is the lifeblood of business and society.

Because its impact is far-reaching, the accounting profession opens vast career possibilities. The in-depth business skills you develop as a CPA prepare you for most positions in management and provide access to the top jobs in business.

CPAs work in a wide variety of arenas: in public practice, in business and industry, in government, and in education. Those in public practice may audit the financial statements of a large Fortune 500 company or advise a small business on a range of subjects vital to the company's survival and growth. They may also serve as personal financial planners, as tax preparers and advisers, and as management and computer consultants. In business, accountants fulfill a wide spectrum of needs from internal auditor to chief financial officer, and from vice president of finance to chief executive officer. In education, accountants serve as professors, department heads, and deans. In government, accountants work at all levels of public service—from the Securities and Exchange Commission and the Internal Revenue Service to financial departments in state and local governments across the land. In these jobs, they advise government leaders, prepare budgets, and develop spending and revenue projections.

Regardless of their job titles, accountants in all fields are charged with keeping the public trust. In fact, the accountant's ultimate responsibility is to serve society by maintaining the highest levels of integrity and objectivity in performing accounting services. As a result, CPAs command a level of trust matched only by a few professions.

Whatever form of practice you choose, accounting provides a challenging and rewarding career in which there are no limits on where you can go, or how far.

—BEATRICE SANDERS
DIRECTOR, ACADEMIC AND CAREER DEVELOPMENT
THE AMERICAN INSTITUTE OF CERTIFIED PUBLIC ACCOUNTANTS

PREFACE

Accounting is an attractive profession because it offers professional challenge, industry diversity, management opportunities, personal growth opportunities, and financial rewards. Major responsibilities of the accountant today are to see that the company complies with government regulations, to advise on how to improve profits and cut losses, to review accounting systems, and to provide outside counsel on management decisions.

The American Institute of Certified Public Accountants (AICPA) publishes an annual study entitled "The Supply of Accounting Graduates and the Demand for Public Accounting Recruits." The 2004 study found that nearly fifty thousand accounting majors graduated in 2003 with B.A.s or M.A.s. Public accounting firms hired 28 percent of new graduates with bachelor's degrees and 59 percent of master's in accounting graduates in 2003. Twenty percent of graduates with bachelor's degrees took jobs in business and industry, as did 18 percent of master's degree graduates. Positions in government were chosen by 4 percent of bachelor's recipients and by 3 percent of graduates with master's degrees. Also in 2003, 109,872 candidates took the CPA exam.

The job outlook is good. The profession is expected to add new jobs at a 10 to 20 percent annual rate, according to the Bureau of Labor Statistics' projections, and since it is such a large profession thousands of replacement jobs will open up each year as current employees retire or move on.

This book will be important to anyone contemplating a career in accounting. It will help the high school student and the beginning accounting student know what to expect in the accounting area. It will help the declared accounting major in college decide whether to enter public accounting, the corporate world, or the governmental area and whether to obtain an advanced degree.

The book has several purposes. One purpose is to guide and inform anyone interested in an accounting career of the many opportunities currently available. Another purpose is to help students plan the necessary steps to achieve success in the field. It also is an aid in career decision making. It will inform students of qualifications needed for different accounting positions and help guidance counselors to advise students.

The book covers accounting careers in public and corporate accounting, governmental and other not-for-profit organizations, and it describes the accounting educator, the self-employed accountant, and the financial planner. Included within each of these career areas are job descriptions of positions, educational qualifications, salary ranges, certification requirements, future job potential, and employment trends.

An entire chapter is included on accounting job opportunities in Canada. This chapter discusses possibilities for employment in public accounting, business and industry, government, and as an accounting educator. Information is included on salary for different categories along with names and addresses of organizations providing certification in different areas of accounting.

There is a chapter on preparing for the accounting job, including a section about college internships, résumé preparation, interviewing, and achieving a professional image. The last chapter gives information needed to advance in a career. It includes ideas on communication, networking, and mentoring.

A suggested reading list of articles and books for additional information is provided at the end of each chapter. Appendixes list names and addresses of professional organizations, addresses of state boards of accountancy, and much more additional useful information. The book provides an in-depth description and discussion of every major area of accounting available for the college graduate.

A thank-you is given to the University of Toledo for hours of typing and to Price Waterhouse for its generous donation of staff time and facilities. A special acknowledgment is made to Paul Bjorn and Donna Murphy in the Cleveland office of Price Waterhouse.

—Gloria L. Gaylord
Glenda E. Ried

 CAREERS in

ACCOUNTING

CHAPTER 1

PUBLIC ACCOUNTING

Accounting theory is shaped by its users and must be flexible to accommodate changing business requirements. From earliest times, people recorded information by making marks on stone or clay. Archaeologists have found evidence of this in the ruins of ancient Sumeria and Egypt.

A late fifteenth-century Italian monk, Luca Pacioli, is credited with the earliest written evidence of double-entry bookkeeping. Today it is possible for a company to keep a complete and coordinated record of all its transactions using a double-entry bookkeeping system. Companies then generate financial statements from this summary of transactions.

The Industrial Revolution began in England in the mid-eighteenth century and spread to the United States during the 1800s. Industrialization required huge amounts of capital and initiated the rise in importance of the corporation as a form of business. The need for a more standard set of accounting rules and regulations that would allow stockholders to compare and evaluate the operations among several companies gave special impetus to the field of public accounting. Public accounting is the area of accounting that is specifically concerned with the preparation and presentation of financial statements in a fair and consistent manner for external use by investors, creditors, and analysts.

Today's accountant is as much a business executive as a technician. The whole nature of the work done by the public accounting profession has undergone some significant changes in recent years, and the changes continue. The requirements for those entering the profession continue to be demanding. The rewards, in terms of remuneration and self-satisfaction, are increasingly attractive.

PRACTICE AREAS

There are five major areas of work within the public accounting field: accounting and auditing, taxation, management consulting, entrepreneurial services, and forensic accounting. In large firms, these areas are separated into different departments. In smaller firms, the areas may not be formally divided because the same person may perform more than one of these functions.

Accounting and Auditing

Accounting and auditing are the basic functions of most public accounting firms and in most large firms still generate a large portion of the firm's revenues.

An auditor's job is to determine whether the economic activities of an organization are fairly reflected in its financial statements. Certified public accountants (CPAs) examine clients' financial statements and express an opinion as to whether these statements fairly present the financial condition of the organization.

Auditors need to go beyond the numbers of a company and look at the operations from a businessperson's perspective. Understanding the total business operation leads to a well-planned and well-executed audit. This includes learning about the company's long-range objectives, strategy, and operating environment, then the systems and procedures that make up its controls, and finally how its people interact with the business and its control systems.

Auditors need to review a company's internal control system. Internal control requires mastery of the methods and procedures that govern the authorization of transactions, the safeguarding of assets, and the accuracy of the financial records. Good internal control aids in maximizing efficiency. It also helps guard against waste, unintentional errors, and fraud.

Auditors examine financial documents and other records. In the past, many pieces of paper had to be examined during the audit, but sophisticated computer systems and advances in technology have forced auditing firms to use state-of-the-art, computer-based automated techniques to per-form many of the audit functions.

Even though many of the functions are computerized, the auditor still needs to confirm bank balances, verify and value ending inventory, check the existence of plant assets, and examine depreciation schedules. The audit involves reading minutes of vital company meetings; studying contracts; and conferring with management, directors, and outside counsel about company operations.

The auditor then reaches a conclusion, using information gained from analyzing the company and from overall knowledge of the business climate. This conclusion is the culmination of the audit work and is called the *audit report*. The independent auditor's act of reporting his or her professional opinion on the fairness of financial statements has come to be known as the *attest function*.

The audit report has a standard three-paragraph format when the state-ments are fairly presented in conformity with "generally accepted account-ing principles." It is as follows:

Independent Auditor's Report

Stockholders and Board of Directors
AU Company

We have audited the accompanying balance sheet of the AU Company as of December 31, 2005, and the related statements of income, retained earnings, and cash flows for the year then ended. These financial state-ments are the responsibility of the Company's management. Our respon-sibility is to express an opinion on these financial statements based on our audit.

We conducted our audit in accordance with generally accepted audit-ing standards. Those standards require that we plan and perform the audit to obtain reasonable assurance about whether the financial state-ments are free of material misstatement. An audit includes examining, on a test basis, evidence supporting the amounts and disclosures in the financial statements. An audit also includes assessing the accounting principles used and significant estimates made by management, as well as evaluating the overall financial statement presentation. We believe that our audit provides a reasonable basis for our opinion.

In our opinion, the financial statements referred to above present fairly, in all material respects, the financial position of AU Company at December 31, 2005, and the results of its operations and its cash flows for the year ended in conformity with generally accepted accounting principles.

Able, Baker, and Charlie
February 15, 2006

The phrase "generally accepted accounting principles" (GAAP) refers to a common set of accounting concepts, standards, and procedures. This set of accounting rules has become generally accepted by agreement and usage.

The American Institute of Certified Public Accountants (AICPA) is a professional organization of CPAs, many of whom are in public accounting practice. The AICPA has been the dominant organization in the development of accounting standards over the last fifty years. From 1939 through 1959, the AICPA Committee on Accounting Procedures issued fifty-one Accounting Research Bulletins (ARBs) recommending certain principles or practices. From 1959 to 1973, the Accounting Principles Board (APB) issued thirty-one Opinions that CPAs are required to follow. In 1973, the APB was replaced by an independent, seven-member, full-time Financial Accounting Standards Board (FASB). The FASB has issued numerous Statements of Financial Accounting Standards and interpretations of those standards. The FASB is widely recognized as the major influence in the private sector in the development of new financial accounting standards.

The Securities and Exchange Commission (SEC), created under the Securities and Exchange Act of 1934, has the authority to prescribe accounting and reporting practices for companies under its jurisdiction. This includes virtually every major U.S. business corporation. Rather than exercise this power, the SEC has adopted a policy of working closely with the accounting profession, especially the FASB, in the development of accounting standards. The SEC indicates to FASB the accounting topics it believes should be addressed. External pressure by the SEC and a concerned public continue to make the FASB a responsible body.

Taxation

Taxation is a complex and challenging area of the accounting profession because of constantly changing tax policies, the growth of multinational firms, and the greater complexity of business in general. Tax-related work forms a significant segment of the practices of both large and small accounting firms. The tax consultant is a crucial resource for businesses and individuals.

The CPA specializing in the tax area offers a broad range of services. These services include tax planning and advice, the filing of tax returns and supporting documents, representation of clients before government agencies, estate planning, and other assistance to clients in regard to complying with tax laws.

The rapid expansion of the complexity and impact of tax problems has increased the demand for tax professionals. Tax advisers often spend much of their time on consulting matters. They are involved in helping executives plan a company's business activity and advising them on personal financial matters.

Typical tax consulting projects include:

- Advising a client on acquisitions and mergers
- Guiding a reorganization of a client's international operations to reduce taxes
- Evaluating tax aspects of various leasing agreements
- Counseling corporate executives on minimizing personal taxes

Since tax laws change often, the tax professional must be a lifelong student in order to remain current and responsive to clients' needs.

Management Consulting Services

The role of management consulting professionals is to help clients define the information needs of their organization and to identify and assemble the data needed to create the information. An important function of management consulting services (MCS) is to help with a company's financial planning and control. Equally important is the area connected with information systems and electronic data processing. Other areas usually handled by MCS are pensions, benefits, and compensation; executive recruiting; operations research and quantitative analysis; and industrial engineering.

The background of the management consulting professional represents a wide range of disciplines, not limited to accounting. Many entry-level consultants have degrees in computer science, general business, or liberal arts (with a quantitative focus on a subject such as math, economics, or statistics).

Some of the largest management consulting organizations in the world operate as departments within accounting firms. Demand for consulting services is international. MCS are used by virtually every industry. Examples of consulting projects by CPA firms are:

- Advised a stock exchange corporation and developed a computer system that improved the speed and accuracy of settlement among brokers
- Assisted New York City in implementing a new integrated financial management system covering all major agencies and programs
- Helped several major railroads with comprehensive resource planning, costing of major operating systems, and rate settlements
- Aided the U.S. Treasury Department in its evaluation of Chrysler Corporation's appeal for financial assistance through financial modeling and a review of financial, marketing, and operating data

A career in management consulting offers the opportunity to work with a company's executives in applying the concepts of modern management and information technology.

Entrepreneurial Services

This is a fast-growing and dynamic practice area that has been formed in most large firms in the last few years. The person working in this area deals with the special requirements of a start-up or growing company. Professionals in this group are involved in counseling and advising the emerging or middle-market company that may lack the in-house resources to successfully handle strategic planning, cost control, attracting capital, going public, or choosing the right information system or compensation plan. Audit, tax, and management consulting skills are all used to satisfy the needs of an emerging business.

Forensic Accounting

Some public accountants specialize in forensic accounting—investigating and interpreting white-collar crimes such as securities fraud and embezzlement, bankruptcies and contract disputes, and other complex and possibly criminal financial transactions, such as money laundering by organized criminals. Forensic accountants combine their knowledge of accounting and finance with law and investigative techniques in order to determine if illegal activity is going on. Many forensic accountants work closely with law enforcement personnel and lawyers during investigations and often appear as expert witnesses during trials.

TYPES OF FIRMS

CPA firms are divided into categories according to such criteria as number of employees, number of offices, or total dollars of billable revenue. Using these criteria, a firm is sometimes classified as small, medium, or large; and local, regional, national, or multinational.

A group of giant multinational CPA firms is known as the Big Four because four firms comprise the group. This group of CPA firms was originally known as the Big Eight; however, a series of mergers in the last two decades have left four organizations to comprise the Big Four. The Big Four firms audit the majority of companies represented in the Fortune 1000. These firms are:

- **Deloitte Touche Tohmatsu.** An organization of member firms providing professional services and advice.
- **Ernst & Young.** Member firms help companies in all industries to handle a broad range of business issues.
- **KPMG.** Provides business advice to help companies manage their businesses.
- **PricewaterhouseCoopers.** Provides assurance, tax, and advisory services to public and private clients.

These CPA firms have offices in many U.S. and Canadian cities, as well as other major cities throughout the world. Addresses of the national headquarters of these firms are listed at the end of this chapter. These four firms have instant name recognition within the accounting profession. Some of the reasons given for choosing a Big Four firm for employment are higher salary, prestige, diversity of clients, and valuable experience. Disadvantages for some people are out-of-town travel, overtime, and the firms' large, impersonal atmosphere.

A regional firm has offices in several states and is well known in the region it serves but may not have the instant national recognition of a Big Four firm. The types of services a regional or middle-sized firm performs and the clients it serves vary greatly, depending on the individual firm.

The category "local firm" usually implies either a single office or a few offices located in neighboring areas. A local firm usually serves small businesses in the town where it is located and those in surrounding areas. A small business may not need the total services required by a large corporation. A company whose stock is not publicly held is not required to secure an audit report certifying that the financial statements are in conformity with GAAP. A compilation or review may be substituted. When an accountant performs a compilation, no opinion or any other assurance of the statements is given. During a review, inquiries and analytical procedures are performed, so the accountant has a reasonable basis for expressing limited assurance about the statements.

When asked the advantages of working in a smaller firm, accountants name diversity of work, less travel, greater independence, better location, and flexible working hours.

LEVELS OF RESPONSIBILITY AND SALARY

Positions of staff rank and levels of responsibility within a typical CPA firm, in ascending order, are (1) staff accountant, (2) senior accountant, (3) manager, and (4) partner. A staff person may work in any of the functional areas of operation: audit, tax, or MCS. Usually, the longer a person stays with a firm, the more specialized his or her knowledge becomes.

The staff accountant usually has up to three years' experience in a firm. The senior accountant represents a range of experience from two to six years. Senior accountants generally supervise several staff accountants.

When an accountant progresses to the level of manager, it means the firm feels the person has the potential to eventually become a partner. The manager level is the first real management position in most firms. Managers often have between five and ten years of experience.

Only about 5 percent of all people entering CPA firms reach the level of partner. It typically takes ten to twelve years for a person to be promoted through the various position ranks to partner. Both responsibility and compensation are increased at this level.

Salaries in accounting firms vary depending on the level of education, locality, size of firm, and whether an accountant has a CPA certificate. The figures in Table 1.1 are excerpted from a 2005 national compensation sur-

Table 1.1 Annual Compensation in Public Accounting Firms

AUDIT, TAX, AND MANAGEMENT SERVICES–LARGE FIRMS ($250 million or more in sales)

Experience/Title	2004	2005
Manager/director	$77,750–$119,000	$81,750–$125,000
Manager	63,000–82,250	68,000–92,000
Senior	48,750–62,250	55,000–69,000
1 to 3 years	41,000–51,250	47,000–55,000
Up to 1 year	35,750–42,500	41,750–47,000

AUDIT, TAX, AND MANAGEMENT SERVICES–MEDIUM FIRMS ($25 to $250 million in sales)

Experience/Title	2004	2005
Manager/director	$68,000–$93,750	$74,000–$107,500
Manager	57,000–74,250	64,500–80,250
Senior	44,000–56,500	48,250–62,000
1 to 3 years	35,250–45,500	42,250–48,000
Up to 1 year	31,750–38,250	35,000–42,000

AUDIT, TAX, AND MANAGEMENT SERVICES–SMALL FIRMS (up to $25 million in sales)

Experience/Title	2004	2005
Manager/director	$63,750–$84,500	$69,000–$87,750
Manager	52,000–66,000	57,750–69,000
Senior	41,000–54,000	45,000–57,000
1 to 3 years	33,750–42,500	38,000–45,000
Up to 1 year	29,500–36,250	34,000–39,250

Source: Robert Half International, Inc., *2005 Salary Guide*. Used by permission.

vey conducted by Robert Half International, Inc., which maintains over three hundred offices worldwide.

Certification in an area, a law degree, or a master's degree may increase the salary figures by 10 to 15 percent. Salaries will also vary according to geographic location.

CERTIFICATION

The professional certifications available to accountants denote educational and professional achievement and a commitment to a code of ethics. Two of the most sought-after designations, Certified Public Accountant (CPA) and public accountant (PA) are detailed here.

Certified Public Accountant

Certified Public Accountant (CPA) is a title conferred upon accountants who meet specified requirements. In the United States, the licensing of accountants is a state function. New York became the first state to sponsor legislation in this area in 1896. Now all fifty states and Guam, Puerto Rico, the Virgin Islands, and Washington, D.C., have boards of accountancy. These boards administer the Uniform CPA Examination on a continual basis two out of every three months throughout the year. For example, in 2005 tests were administered in January and February, April and May, July and August, and October and November. Detailed information about test scheduling is available from the AICPA (see Appendix A).

The Board of Examiners of the American Institute of Certified Public Accountants (AICPA) is responsible for preparation of the Uniform CPA Examination and the Advisory Grading Service. Over one hundred thousand candidates sit for the test each year.

The primary objective of the Uniform CPA Examination is to test the candidate's professional competence in the discipline of accounting. It also tests the ability to apply knowledge skillfully and with good judgment and an understanding of professional responsibility. In early 2004 the exam became fully computerized, requiring applicants to possess basic computer skills and search abilities. The revised computer-based CPA Examination is a fourteen-hour test with four sections: Auditing and Attestation; Busi-

ness Environment and Concepts; Financial Accounting and Reporting; and
Regulation.

The sections of the revised Uniform CPA exam are described as follows
by the AICPA:

Auditing and Attestation
1. Planning the engagement
2. Internal controls
3. Obtain and document information
4. Review engagement and evaluate information
5. Prepare communications

Business Environment and Concepts
1. Business structure
2. Economic concepts
3. Financial management
4. Information technology
5. Planning and measurement

Financial Accounting and Reporting
1. Concepts and standards for financial statements
2. Typical items in financial statements
3. Specific types of transactions and events
4. Accounting and reporting for governmental entities
5. Accounting and reporting for nongovernmental and not-for-
   profit organizations

Regulation
1. Ethics and professional responsibility
2. Business law
3. Federal tax procedures and accounting issues
4. Federal taxation of property transactions
5. Federal taxation—individuals
6. Federal taxation—entities

Since each state has its own board of accountancy, examination standards and licensing requirements vary. Requirements include education,

years of experience, state residency, application filing dates, and fees. All states require a prospective CPA to pass the Uniform CPA Examination, although no state requires that all parts be passed at one time. An ethics exam is required in many states after the four parts of the Uniform CPA Examination have been passed. Usually the ethics exam is an open-book test and is not difficult to pass. There are reciprocity agreements between states so that a person who has passed all or part of the CPA Examination can be given credit if the person moves to another state. Complete information regarding each jurisdiction's requirements for CPA candidates is available at cpa-exam.org. Select the link "Getting Started" and proceed to "Steps to Becoming a CPA." An interactive map allows users to select a state and study its requirements.

The revised computer-based examination includes multiple-choice questions and case studies called *simulations*. The multiple-choice portion of the examination is presented as sequential testlets, which are groups of questions designed to appear together. Each exam section includes approximately three multiple-choice testlets; each testlet contains twenty-four to thirty questions. Each exam section, except Business Environment and Concepts, also includes two simulations. Simulations are condensed case studies designed to test candidates' accounting knowledge and skills using real life work-related situations. Each simulation is approximately thirty to fifty minutes in length and complements the multiple-choice portion of the examination. All simulations are intended to assess knowledge and skills that are appropriate to expect of an entry-level accountant.

As of early 2003, based on recommendations made by the AICPA, forty-two states and the District of Columbia require CPA candidates to complete 150 semester hours of college coursework—an additional thirty hours beyond the usual four-year bachelor's degree. Another five states—Arizona, Minnesota, New Mexico, New York, and Virginia—have adopted similar legislation that will become effective between 2004 and 2009. Colorado, Delaware, New Hampshire, and Vermont are the only states that do not require 150 semester hours. Many schools have altered their curricula accordingly with most programs offering masters degrees as part of the 150 hours, and prospective accounting majors should carefully research accounting curricula and the requirements of any states in which they hope to become licensed.

Detailed information about the Uniform CPA Examination and continuing education requirements is available from the AICPA. Visit the organization's website at aicpa.org. The site offers sample tests, an information video, and much more information for the prospective test taker.

Specific state requirements can be obtained from the state's board of accountancy. The address and website of each state board are listed in Appendix C.

Certification is an important goal of many people graduating from college with a major or concentration in accounting. Advantages of certification frequently include increased professional status, extra compensation, promotion, and personal satisfaction.

A licensed CPA has the option of joining the AICPA, the national organization of CPAs. Each state, as well as Guam, Puerto Rico, the Virgin Islands, and the District of Columbia, has its own society of CPAs, which a licensed CPA may join. The professional organizations provide CPAs a chance to grow professionally and meet new people. State societies offer continuing education programs to update knowledge. (See Appendix A for a list of names and addresses of national headquarters of accounting-related organizations.)

State CPA Examination Conditioning Requirements. The Uniform CPA Examination is administered in four sections: Auditing and Attestation; Business Environment and Concepts; Financial Accounting and Reporting; and Regulation. Each section is graded separately, but a candidate must pass all sections with a score of 75 or higher in order to be eligible to become a CPA.

Because the examination is so rigorous, few candidates are able to pass all sections the first time they take them. However, boards of accountancy may award credit to candidates who earn passing grades in some sections while failing to qualify in others. Under such circumstances, the board is said to grant the candidate *conditional status*. The rules for earning conditional status are known as *conditioning requirements*, and they vary from state to state.

In general, most boards require candidates to pass at least two sections before they can achieve conditional status, although a few boards grant conditional status to candidates who pass only one section. In addition, many boards also require candidates to earn a minimum grade in the sections failed in order for the candidates to receive credit for the sections passed. Candidates with conditional status are usually given a specific number of additional opportunities to pass the remaining sections, after which conditional credit expires and candidates must retake those sections. In most jurisdictions, candidates are required to take all sections of the examination for which credit has not been awarded, so candidates taking the examination for the first time must take all four sections.

Contact your state's board of accountancy for specific conditioning requirements.

Public Accountant

Most states specify certain requirements for a person to be licensed as a public accountant (PA) or an accounting practitioner (AP), and it is illegal to represent oneself as a PA or AP without the proper license. Continuing professional education is also a common requirement. The states set their own criteria for public accountants, and information on licensing may be obtained from the states' Boards of Accountancy, listed in Appendix C.

Licensing requirements for a PA or AP are not as rigid or as difficult as for a CPA license. The continuing professional education (CPE) requirements for PAs or APs vary from 0 to 120 hours every three years. Courses that qualify for credit are similar to those for CPAs, and most states require CPE for renewal of a public accountant license.

EMPLOYMENT OPPORTUNITIES

The following advertisements are typical of those that appear in the *Wall Street Journal* or other business publications.

Management Advisory Services—Consulting Positions

A growing and dynamic public accounting firm is looking for experienced consultants for several of our Midwestern, Rocky Mountain, and Southwestern locations. To help us accomplish our ambitious goals and meet the needs of our clients, we need highly motivated self-starters with excellent interpersonal and communication skills. Candidates should have a strong orientation toward client service and desire to provide clients with substantive business advice. Requirements for these positions include:

- Four to six years of consulting experience in a major CPA firm
- Knowledge of general accounting and EDP systems
- A bachelor's degree in accounting or related business area; CPA and advanced degree a plus

Salary depends upon background and experience, plus full benefits and an environment conducive to personal and professional growth.

Accountants—CPA Firm

A growing and dynamic public accounting firm is looking for experienced staff accountants for several of our Midwestern, Rocky Mountain, and Southwestern locations. If you have an interest in joining our select team of experienced professionals providing accounting, auditing, and tax compliance services to a widely diversified clientele, we may have an opening for you. Candidates must have:

- Two to five years of experience in auditing with large public accounting firm
- Degree in accounting; CPA and advanced degree a plus
- Excellent communication and interpersonal skills with a strong orientation toward client service

Our firm has the resources of a large organization yet offers the small firm environment that is conducive to personal and professional development. If you are highly motivated and a self-starter, you can help us achieve our ambitious goals and meet the needs of our clients.

Tax Professionals

A national CPA firm is seeking highly motivated and technically qualified CPAs to expand our tax services area.

Our growth plans require professional tax consultants for senior, supervisor, and manager positions. Candidates should have a minimum three to six years of broad tax experience and a desire to work with our diverse clientele.

Our training programs, professional environment, and diversified tax services offer you the opportunity to reach successively higher levels of professionalism. We also offer a highly competitive compensation and benefits package.

Accountants—Audit/Tax MCS

A national CPA firm is seeking individuals at all levels with current or recent public accounting experience to join its rapidly expanding coast-to-coast practice. Interested applicants should be committed to public accounting as a career and partnership as a goal. Excellent opportunities are available.

Ours is a broadly diversified national and international clientele. Our people learn through close association with the firm's top professionals and by participating in our extensive continuing professional education program. We provide top fringe benefits and an income level that recognizes your talents. We would like to introduce you to an exciting future.

Local CPA Firm

Local CPA firm that is expanding into a regional firm has an opening for a strongly motivated individual with two to five years' experience in public accounting. Excellent partnership opportunities are available as a result of our growth and our in-house CPE program.

Most firms look for the same qualities in a prospective employee: technical ability, motivation, leadership skills, and personality. Much time and money are spent on recruiting by most accounting firms.

Accounting firms will usually have representatives on campus to recruit interested students. The initial interview may only last half an hour. Approximately 20 to 25 percent of the students interviewed on campus will receive invitations for a more extensive interview at the CPA firm's office. About half the office interviews culminate in a job offer.

The college placement office is probably the best source of information about the interviewing and recruiting process of the CPA firms. Of course, it is always appropriate to write directly to the specific firm in which you are interested.

The AICPA publishes an annual study on the supply of accounting graduates and the demand for public accounting recruits. According to the 2004 survey, 49,665 accounting degrees were awarded in the 2002–2003 academic year, representing a growth rate of 11 percent. A total of 37,010 bachelor's degrees and 12,655 master's degrees were awarded. In addition, 145 doctorates were awarded in accounting, representing a growth rate of 32 percent.[1]

CPA firms hired 13,270 graduates with bachelor's degrees in 2003. A total of 3,555 master's degree holders were hired. These figures represent increases of 5 percent for undergraduates and 8 percent for graduate degrees.[2]

NATIONAL OFFICES OF THE BIG FOUR FIRMS

Deloitte Touche Tohmatsu
1633 Broadway
New York, NY 10019
deloitte.com

Ernst & Young
1211 Avenue of the Americas
New York, NY 10036
ey.com

KPMG
345 Park Avenue
New York, NY 10154
kpmg.com

PricewaterhouseCoopers LLC
300 Madison Avenue, 24th Floor
New York, NY 10017
pwcglobal.com

NOTES

1. Sanders, Beatrice, and Leticia B. Romeo, *The Supply of Accounting Graduates and the Demand for Public Accounting Recruits—2004*, American Institute of Certified Public Accountants, aicpa.org (visited June 22, 2005).
2. Ibid.

SUGGESTED READING

AICPA. *Information for Uniform CPA Candidates.* 17th ed. New York: AICPA.

AICPA. *Information for International Uniform CPA Qualification Examination Candidates (IQEX).* 3rd ed. New York: AICPA.

Bragg, Steven M. *Accounting Best Practices.* 3rd ed. New York: Wiley, 2003.

Reports published by any of the large accounting firms explaining their philosophies and policies.

Robert Half International, Inc. *2005 Salary Guide for Accounting, Finance and Information Technology.* Published annually. Menlo Park, CA: Robert Half International, Inc., 2005.

Robert Half International, Inc. *Glossary of Job Descriptions for Accounting and Finance.* Menlo Park, CA: Robert Half International, Inc.

Sanders, Beatrice, and Leticia B. Romeo. *The Supply of Accounting Graduates and the Demand for Public Accounting Recruits.* New York: AICPA, 2004.

CHAPTER

CORPORATE ACCOUNTING

Above all, businesses strive to maximize long-run profits and reduce short-term debt. One of the sound management practices needed to reach these objectives is the company's accounting system.

The accounting department must be designed to meet the needs and characteristics of the particular business of which it is a part. For this reason, no single information system design is superior for all types of businesses.

CORPORATE JOB TITLES AND RESPONSIBILITIES

A financial organizational structure adopted by many corporations has a vice president–finance or chief financial officer (CFO) in charge of all financial operations. The positions reporting to the CFO are generally the treasurer and controller. A typical structure of this type is illustrated in Figure 2.1.

It is important to realize that job titles frequently vary among corporations. A divisional controller in one organization may be an accounting manager, an assistant controller, or a plant accountant in another. In industrial accounting, position responsibility rather than position title determines what functions and activities will be performed.

Vice President–Finance or Chief Financial Officer (CFO)

Long-term financing decisions are made only once every few years in most companies, but these decisions have a large impact on the firm's success

Figure 2.1

An Organizational Structure for Corporate Financial Functions

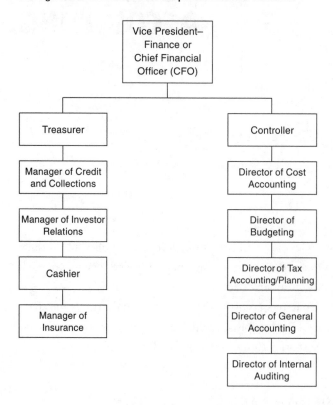

and growth over that period. Success depends on making the right decisions about timing and sources of funds. Timing is important because the CFO has little control over the economy, an external variable that can influence stock and bond prices, interest rates, and capital markets in general. Therefore, the CFO must try to stabilize the flow of funds to ensure availability when needed. Alternative choices for sources of funding include the issuance of common stock, preferred stock, or bonds.

The dividend policy of the company is important because many stockholders consider the stability and amount of dividend before buying stock. The policy is also related to long-term financing because the smaller the dividend, the more cash a company will retain for paying bills.

The CFO also directs and supervises the work of the controller and treasurer and has administrative responsibility for the personnel and performance of these departments. The CFO advises the president of the organization on matters concerning financial reporting, financial stability, and liquidity. The CFO typically bears the responsibility for maintaining close contact with stockholders, the investment community, and financial institutions.

Often the CFO is a member of the corporation's executive committee and participates in planning and policy decisions. By the time a person attains the position of CFO, he or she will usually have had fifteen to twenty years of experience in the field of business. Most CFOs hold a bachelor's degree in accounting or finance, and many also have a master's degree in business.

Treasurer

The treasurer receives, disburses, and protects the company's cash; invests surplus funds; and manages pension and trust funds. The treasurer also determines the optimal cash position for the organization, governs overall credit policy, investigates insurance coverage, negotiates loans, and maintains banking relationships.

In a small company, some of the duties of the treasurer's office are combined and performed by a few employees. In a large company, typically each department has a separate staff. A medium-sized company may have some departments fully staffed, while other departments may be combined.

• Manager of credit and collections. The manager of credit and collections reports to the treasurer and has the responsibility of developing and administering the credit and collection policy. The policies must be tight enough to assure minimum bad debt expense, but loose enough to avoid loss of sales and customers.

• Manager of investor relations. The manager of investor relations has the responsibility of developing and maintaining a market for the company's securities. This includes communication with stockholders, security analysts, and investment bankers.

• Cashier. The duties of a cashier are more administrative than policy-making. The cashier is responsible for endorsing checks, depositing cash, and maintaining a record of cash receipts and disbursements. These duties also could include maintaining banking arrangements for the company.

• Manager of insurance. In a large company, the manager of insurance heads a separate department responsible for the firm's insurance coverage, including the bonding of employees. This department evaluates all tangible assets, including buildings, equipment, and inventories, and determines the adequate level of insurance for them. Identification of potential losses and risks should be discussed with management. The insurance department evaluates the amount of life insurance and professional liability insurance coverage the company needs to carry on key employees.

Controller

The controller is the chief accounting executive and is a participant in top-level decision making affecting the company. This includes developing forecasts, measuring actual performance against expected results, and interpreting data. The controllership function normally includes responsibility for all financial and managerial accounting and reporting. Financial accounting involves reporting to stockholders, creditors, and investors. Managerial accounting concerns compiling and reporting figures, such as budgets, production reports, and cost variances, for internal use.

The controller guides and supervises the work of the managers in charge of the departments of cost, budgeting, tax planning, general accounting, and, sometimes, the internal audit department. The controllership position requires an in-depth understanding of the general business environment in addition to knowledge in the accounting and finance areas.

Cost accounting. Cost accounting involves developing and modifying a cost accounting system that is tailored to meet the informational needs of management. In a manufacturing firm, the cost accounting department should work closely with production management. Output from the cost accounting department typically includes timely, accurate reports on labor, material, overhead charges (both fixed and variable), and product costing. A review of the allocation of overhead costs should be done periodically.

Most companies employ a standard cost system that uses the standard material and labor requirements developed by the company's production engineering department. A standard cost per unit is calculated which can be compared to actual costs per unit. Differences between the actual cost of production and the standard or expected cost are called *variances*. Any variances of a significant dollar amount are investigated and explained. This is an example of management by exception and provides important feedback to the various departments on their performance.

The cost accounting department also becomes involved in developing studies of future projects, such as building a new manufacturing plant or warehouse.

Budgeting. Most companies have written goals and objectives. When these goals and objectives are expressed in financial terms, the document is called a *budget*. Budgeting includes the preparation of operational budgets, capital budgets, and cash budgets.

The preparation of company budgets is the responsibility of the controller's staff, but the process requires input from additional personnel from the production, marketing, and operating areas. An annual operating budget for a business organization starts with a sales forecast. This forecast is used to project a sales budget, which is segregated by product and division within the company. The sales forecast is also used to prepare a production budget. A budget predicting the amount of raw materials to be purchased and labor that will be needed is also generated. The operating budget forecasts operating revenue, expenses, and the expected net income.

Capital budgets show how and where a company plans to spend funds for large plant and equipment items and for long-term projects.

Cash budgeting is a forecast estimating cash inflow and outflow for a month or longer. This is important to a company as an aid in determining whether it will be able to pay short-term bills or if it needs to look for sources of short-term financing.

Tax accounting/planning. The responsibilities of this department include the reporting and timely filing of all federal, state, and local income tax returns. The department must also comply with all necessary reports for the Securities and Exchange Commission. These reports must be filed by all corporations whose stock is publicly traded.

This department conducts research in the following areas:

- Buying and selling fixed assets
- Acquiring and/or selling subsidiaries
- Investment tax credits

- Issuing and retiring bonds or stock
- Purchasing and/or selling investment securities
- Foreign tax calculations

After initial research is completed on tax planning, the executive committee usually makes final decisions on tax matters. The company's tax accounting department generally seeks advice on any unusual or complicated matters from the tax department of the independent financial accounting firm that performs its audit. (See Chapter 1 for a detailed discussion of accounting firms.)

General accounting. The general accounting functions of most companies are now computerized. These functions include:

- Journalizing. Records the everyday transactions.
- Payroll. Maintains employee payroll records and prepares paychecks.
- Billing. Sends out statements.
- General ledger area. Maintains balance sheet and income statement accounts.
- Accounts payable. Authorizes and disburses payment.

The international accounting function is usually in the general accounting area for companies that have a need for such a department. The responsibilities of international accounting include foreign currency translations and the resulting effects on the company's books, consolidating foreign subsidiaries, and any other related effects on the parent company.

Internal auditing. The responsibilities of internal auditing include:

- Independent appraisal of the performance of various levels of management with regard to efficiency and adherence to company policies
- Continuous review and recommendations for improvements in a system of internal checks and protective measures in the organization
- Periodic assessment of the reliability of financial records and effectiveness of processing methods

Congress passed the Foreign Corrupt Practices Act in 1977. This bill requires companies to maintain and comply with an adequate system of internal accounting controls. Since the law was passed, internal auditing staffs have grown in size, and some companies that did not have audit staffs have since established them.

The scope of internal auditors' responsibilities has broadened in the last three decades, leading to increased contact with the senior levels of management. As many corporate operations become larger and more complex, it is not possible for top-level executives to have direct control over all activities. Many potential problems are identified before they reach serious proportions by using the internal audit staff to evaluate financial and nonfinancial controls and to test the company's compliance with them.

The function and role of the internal auditor was for a long time similar to that of the external financial auditor: attesting to the accuracy of the financial statements. Recent years have seen a shift to internal auditors devoting more than half of their time to nonfinancial audits, commonly referred to as operational or management audits, which cover all areas of a company's operations. The purpose of operational audits is to identify areas of operational efficiency that need improvement.

Certified Fraud Examiner (CFE)

In the last decade, a growing number of corporations have been defendants in suits brought by stockholders. The stockholder may allege mismanagement of funds or accuse the company of fraud. Fraud will never be completely eradicated, but it usually can be uncovered, controlled, or abated.

The Association of Certified Fraud Examiners confers the Certified Fraud Examiner (CFE) designation to denote expertise in fraud prevention, detection, and investigation of fraud that is committed by business and government employees.

The CFE exam is administered by computer, making it convenient for test-takers to schedule the exam. It includes five hundred true/false and objective questions that cover the following areas:

- **Criminology and ethics.** Administration of criminal justice, theories of crime causation, theories of fraud prevention, crime information sources, and ethical situations.

- **Financial transactions.** Basic accounting and auditing theory, fraud schemes, internal controls to deter fraud, and other auditing and accounting matters.
- **Fraud investigation.** Interviewing, taking statements, obtaining information from public records, tracing illicit transactions, evaluating deception, and report writing.
- **Legal elements of fraud.** The legal ramifications of conducting fraud examinations, including criminal and civil law, rules of evidence, rights of the accused and accuser, and expert witness matters.

The CFE exam is completed in a total of 10 hours. Each section is allocated a maximum of 2.5 hours to complete. Each of the four exam sections has 125 questions; a maximum of 75 seconds is allowed to answer each question. Candidates must complete all sections in thirty days. A score of at least 75 percent correct answers in every section is required to pass the exam.

More information about the CFE exam can be obtained by contacting:

Certified Fraud Examiner Program
Association of Certified Fraud Examiners
World Headquarters, The Gregor Building
716 West Avenue
Austin, TX 78701
cfenet.com/cfe

EDUCATION AND SALARY

The following advertisements, taken from various business publications, list typical job descriptions for various accounting positions available in the corporate world.

Controller

Manufacturer of small metal parts has an opening for a controller. Degreed and CPA. Must be experienced with financial reporting, costs, data processing, credit and collection, and all general accounting. Job will require hands-on experience with all duties, in addition to strong supervisory skills. Excellent opportunity with a quality company to replace retiring incumbent. Salary open.

Staff Accountant

Entry-level accounting position. Responsibilities include translating foreign currencies, intercompany reconciliations, and account analysis. Requires a degree in accounting, no experience necessary.

Cost Accountant (Accounting or Finance)

Positions involve performing accounting analysis, establishing controls, documenting internal standard procedures, generating reports, preparing month-end closing entries, interfacing with various functional disciplines (i.e., production, materials, industrial engineering), and programming and developing timesharing internal systems and report mechanisms.

EDP Auditors

Bachelor's degree in accounting, business administration, or information science preferred. Master's degree desirable. Certified internal auditor or certified internal system auditor desirable. Two to four years' internal audit or EDP audit experience. Above average written and oral communication skills required.

Accounting Analyst

Bachelor's degree in accounting, two to three years of experience, at least one year in cost accounting; systems knowledge, preferably some academic experience coupled with hands-on systems experience. Background in standard/process cost systems, general accounting, reconciliations, inventory, month-end closings, and standard revisions.

Cost/Budget Supervisor

A four-year degree and a minimum of three years of manufacturing cost experience and general accounting exposure is necessary. Excellent room for growth with this national company. Good benefits.

Accounts Payable

Local growth-oriented firm seeking individual with minimum two years of accounts payable experience. Knowledge of data entry and basic accounting essential. Past experience with a medium or large size company desirable. Salary $18,000 to $20,000 per year depending on experience, plus benefits.

Of the job categories described earlier in the chapter, entry-level jobs for credit and collection, cashier, and general accounting frequently do not require a college degree. As the preceding advertisements state, some accounting background is helpful in securing a job. Unfortunately, little or no education equates with low-paying jobs. Some entry-level jobs not requiring a college degree list salaries in the mid- to high teens.

In larger firms, many of the job categories described in this chapter have junior, senior, and manager levels. The junior level typically requires up to a three-year stay to gain experience and to learn company operations and procedures before promotion to the senior level. In most companies, the junior level requires a degree with an emphasis in accounting or finance.

Senior level in a corporate job usually requires from two to six years of experience with increasing responsibilities and includes the supervision of one or more junior accountants. A bachelor's degree in accounting or finance is usually required, and many senior accountants have earned a master's degree.

Being promoted to the manager level is a crucial, important step in an accountant's career for several reasons. This level represents the first line of management, and it is critical for advancement in the company. A person in the manager position usually reports directly to the treasurer or controller. At this level, most persons have already become certified in their chosen field.

Controller or treasurer is the next promotion available. Few employees in a company reach this level. This job category usually means that the accountant has fifteen or more years of experience, bachelor's and master's degrees, and certification. Reaching this level involves acceptance in the inner circle of top management.

Chief financial officer is the position with the highest level of responsibility and achievement within the financial function of an industrial organization. The job description of the CFO was discussed earlier in the chapter.

The salary figures in Tables 2.1 and 2.2 for various financial positions have been excerpted from a report compiled by Robert Half International, Inc.

Certification in an area, a law degree, or a master's degree may increase the salary figures by 10 to 15 percent. Salaries will also vary according to geographic location.

Table 2.1 Corporate Financial Salaries

CFO AND TREASURER

Company $ Volume in Millions	2004	2005
$500+	$244,000–$346,750	$244,500–$347,000
$250 to $500	170,750–230,750	170,250–231,250
$100 to $250	111,500–153,500	111,750–153,250
$50 to $100	92,750–122,500	92,750–122,500
−$50	84,250–110,750	84,500–111,000

CONTROLLER

Company $ Volume in Millions	2004	2005
$500+	$104,250–$145,750	$105,750–$147,250
$250 to $500	95,500–128,000	95,000–129,000
$100 to $250	80,500–107,250	81,000–106,750
$50 to $100	68,750–87,250	68,500–87,750
−$50	61,250–73,500	61,250–73,500

ASSISTANT CONTROLLER AND ASSISTANT TREASURER

Company $ Volume in Millions	2004	2005
$500+	$89,250–$113,000	$89,750–$114,750
$250 to $500	77,750–97,000	77,500–97,750
$100 to $250	65,750–83,500	66,250–84,000
$50 to $100	56,500–72,500	56,750–72,250
−$50	43,750–66,250	44,500–65,750

TAX MANAGER

Company $ Volume in Millions	2004	2005
$250+	$77,250–$114,000	$78,000–$113,750
$50 to $250	64,000–85,000	64,000–85,500

Source: Robert Half International, Inc., *2005 Salary Guide*. Used by permission.

Table 2.2 Bookkeeper and Clerk Salaries in All Companies

Title	2004	2005
Full Charge (Financial Statements)	$32,500–$41,500	$33,500–$43,250
Full Charge (General Ledger)	30,000–36,250	30,750–37,750
Billing Manager	33,000–42,500	34,000–43,750
Bookkeeper	25,000–31,000	26,250–32,750
Accounting Clerk	25,000–31,000	24,250–30,750

Source: Robert Half International, Inc., *2005 Salary Guide*. Used by permission.

CERTIFICATION

Certification denotes educational and professional excellence, and can enhance one's career potential. Four of the designations sought by those working in corporate accounting—Certified Management Accountant (CMA), Certified Financial Manager (CFM), Certified Internal Auditor (CIA), and Certified Information Systems Auditor (CISA)—are described here.

Certified Management Accountant

In response to the needs of business and at the request of many in the academic community, the Institute of Management Accountants (IMA) established a program to recognize professional competence and educational attainment in management accounting. This recently revised program culminates in the designation of Certified Management Accountant (CMA).

The CMA program requires candidates to pass a series of uniform examinations and to meet specific educational and professional standards to qualify for and maintain the CMA. The IMA has established the Institute of Certified Management Accountants (ICMA) to administer the program, conduct the examinations, and grant certificates to those who qualify.

The objectives of the program are fourfold:

• To establish management accounting as a recognized profession by identifying the role of the management accountant and financial

manager, the underlying body of knowledge, and a course of study
by which such knowledge is acquired.

- To encourage higher educational standards in the management
  accounting field.
- To establish an objective measure of an individual's knowledge and
  competence in the field of management accounting.
- To encourage continued professional development by management
  accountants.

Candidates for the CMA must apply to the Institute of Certified Management Accounting. Admission to the ICMA and the CMA program
require the applicant to be of good moral character, to be employed or
expect to be employed in the management accounting area, to be a member of IMA, and to satisfy one of the following conditions:

- Hold a baccalaureate degree in any area from an accredited college
  or university.
- Be a certified public accountant or hold a professional qualification
  similar to the CPA or CMA, issued in a foreign country.
- Achieve a score in the fiftieth percentile or higher on either the
  Graduate Management Admissions Test (GMAT) or the Graduate
  Record Examination (GRE).
- Candidates holding a degree from an accredited foreign institution
  must submit a transcript translated into English, showing the
  official university seal. A notarized translation is acceptable.

The CMA examination is a comprehensive four-part exam designed to
measure an individual's knowledge and competence in the practice of management accounting and financial management. The examination questions
are constructed to measure technical knowledge and to assess the individual's ability to analyze information and communicate the results in a mean-
ingful and understandable manner.

Parts 1, 2, and 3 of the exam are 100 percent objective and consist of
carefully constructed multiple-choice questions that test all levels of cog-
nitive skills. Part 4 consists of several essay questions and problems that are
delivered in a computer-based format. Both written and quantitative
responses will be required.

The computer-generated exams are offered daily (except Sundays and holidays) at testing centers throughout the United States and internationally. After registration for Parts 1, 2, and 3 with the ICMA, candidates are assigned a 120-day period in which to schedule the examination with the test administration vendor. Candidates are allowed one month from the date of registration for Part 4 to take that exam.

Recognizing that successful completion of the requirements for other rigorous professional accounting and financial certification programs demonstrates a candidate's competence in business analysis, the ICMA Board of Regents will grant a waiver of Part 1 for those candidates who have earned certain other certifications. To be granted the waiver, acceptable proof must be supplied to ICMA along with the appropriate waiver fee. Acceptable designations include Chartered Financial Analyst (CFA), CFA Institute; Certified Internal Auditor (CIA), Institute of Internal Auditors; and Certified Public Accountant (CPA), American Institute of Certified Public Accountants. Acceptable Canadian designations include Chartered Accountant (CA), Canadian Institute of Chartered Accountants; Certified General Accountant (CGA), Certified General Accountants' Association of Canada; and Certified Management Accountant (CMA), Society of Management Accountants of Canada.

Certified Financial Manager

The Certified Financial Manager (CFM) certification provides ICMA members who are involved with corporate cash management, financing and investment decisions, and risk management with a means for further demonstrating an expanded skill set. This exam provides an in-depth measure of competence in areas such as financial statement analysis, working capital policy, capital structure, valuation issues, and risk management.

Those candidates who have completed all four parts of the CMA program can take Part 2CFM to become a CFM. The general content of the exam is as follows:

1. Financial statement analysis (15–25 percent)
2. Working capital policy and management (15–20 percent)
3. Strategic issues in finance (15–25 percent)
4. Risk management (15–25 percent)

5. External financial environment (15–20 percent)
6. Employee benefit plans (5–10 percent)

The requirements for the CFM are identical to those for the CMA designation.

Continuing professional education. Candidates who have successfully completed all parts of the certification program must maintain their professional competence through a regular program of continuing professional education. To remain in good standing with the Institute of Certified Management Accountants the following are required:

- Thirty hours of continuing education must be completed each calendar year subsequent to passing the exam.
- Reporting of continuing education is done in conjunction with renewal of IMA membership.
- Credit will be given for subjects relevant to the CMA's or CFM's career development and related to employer needs. Such qualifying subjects include management accounting, financial management, corporate taxation, computer science, systems analysis, statistics, management skills, insurance, marketing, and business law.
- CMAs can earn thirty hours of continuing education credit for successfully completing Part 2CFM; likewise, CFMs can earn thirty hours for completing Part 2CMA.

Programs sponsored by educational organizations, employers, business organizations, and professional and trade associations at the local or national level qualify for CPE credit. Programs may be in the form of courses, seminars, workshops, technical meetings, or self-study packages. Technical speeches and published articles will also be considered for continuing education credit.

For further information about the CMA and CFM programs, contact:

Institute of Certified Management Accountants
10 Paragon Drive
Montvale, NJ 07645
imanet.org

Certified Internal Auditor

In 1941 a group of dedicated internal auditors in New York City decided they needed a professional organization that could represent their profession, develop the professional status of internal auditing, and provide for the interchange of ideas and information among practicing auditors. They founded the Institute of Internal Auditors (IIA), the recognized professional organization for internal auditors.

The Certified Internal Auditors (CIA) Examination is sponsored by the IIA and was first administered in August 1974. The four-part exam is offered twice a year, in May and November, and it is given over two consecutive days at testing locations throughout the United States and internationally. Candidates may choose to take one or more exam parts at any time during the program eligibility period, and in any order of preference. For example, a candidate may elect to begin by taking Part 3 and then proceed to take other parts. Another candidate may elect to take Parts 1 and 2 during one exam cycle and then the remaining parts at a later date. Or a candidate may choose to take all four parts during one exam cycle. The choice is yours to make.

To be eligible to take the CIA exam, candidates must hold a bachelor's degree or its equivalent from an accredited college-level institution. Work experience will not substitute for an appropriate degree.

The IIA will accept student candidates into the CIA program who are: (1) enrolled as a senior in an undergraduate program or as a graduate student; (2) full-time students as defined by the institution in which the student is enrolled (a minimum of twelve semester hours or its equivalent is required for undergraduate students and nine semester hours for graduate students); and (3) register for and take the CIA exam while enrolled in school.

CIA candidates must complete twenty-four months of internal auditing experience or its equivalent, which means experience in audit/assessment disciplines, including external auditing, quality assurance, compliance, and internal control. A master's degree or work experience in related business professions (such as accounting, law, or finance) can be substituted for one year of experience. Candidates may sit for the CIA exam prior to satisfying the professional experience requirement, but they will not be certified until the experience requirement has been met.

Each section of the CIA exam consists of 125 multiple-choice questions. A general breakdown of the exam is as follows:

Part 1: Internal Audit in Governance, Risk, and Control
Comply with IIA attribute standards (15–25 percent)
Establish a risk-based plan to determine priorities of the audit (15–25
    percent)
Understand the audit's role in organizational governance (10–20
    percent)
Perform other internal audit roles and responsibilities (0–10 percent)
Governance, risk, and control knowledge elements (15–25 percent)
Plan engagements (15–25 percent)

Part 2: Conducting the Internal Audit Engagement
Conduct engagements (25–35 percent)
Conduct specific engagements (25–35 percent)
Monitor engagement outcomes (5–15 percent)
Fraud knowledge elements (5–15 percent)
Engagement tools (15–25 percent)

Part 3: Business Analysis and Information Technology
Business processes (15–25 percent)
Financial accounting and finance (15–25 percent)
Managerial accounting (10–20 percent)
Regulatory, legal, and economics (5–15 percent)
Information technology (30–40 percent)

Part 4: Business Management Skills
Strategic management (20–30 percent)
Global business environments (15–25 percent)
Organizational behavior (15–25 percent)
Management skills (20–30 percent)
Negotiating (5–15 percent)

Upon certification, CIAs are required to maintain their knowledge and
skills and to stay abreast of improvements and current developments in
internal auditing standards, procedures, and techniques. Practicing CIAs
must complete and report eighty hours of continuing professional education (CPE) every two years.
For further information concerning the CIA, contact:

The CIA Program
The Institute of Internal Auditors
249 Maitland Avenue
Altamonte Springs, FL 32701-4201
theiia.org

Certified Information Systems Auditor

Most of today's business applications involve data processing. As a result of the growing complexity of systems, electronic data processing (EDP) auditors are now called information systems auditors. The prerequisites for a well-controlled information system are:

- Properly trained data processing technicians who have a knowledge of controls
- Users and managers who understand systems development

The Information Systems Audit and Control Association (ISACA) confers the designation of Certified Information Systems Auditor (CISA), which denotes excellence in information systems (IS) auditing, control, and security. To qualify for CISA certification, candidates must pass the CISA exam, have a minimum of five years IS auditing, control, or security work experience, uphold the ISACA code of professional ethics, and meet continuing education requirements.

The CISA exam is offered twice a year, in June and December, at various locations throughout the United States and internationally. The exam consists of two hundred multiple-choice questions, administered over four hours, and it covers:

- The IS audit process
- Management, planning, and organization of IS
- Technical infrastructure and operational practices
- Protection of information assets
- Disaster recovery and business continuity
- Business application system development, acquisition, implementation, and maintenance
- Business process evaluation and risk management

The CISA continuing professional education policy requires the attainment of continuing professional education (CPE) hours over an annual and three-year certification period. In order to maintain certification, CISAs must complete a minimum of 20 CPE hours annually, and 120 hours over a three-year period.

For further information about CISA, contact:

Information Systems Audit and Control Association
3701 Algonquin Road, Suite 1010
Rolling Meadows, IL 60008
isaca.org

THE FUTURE

It is estimated that more than 60 percent of all accountants work in some area of corporate business, and many experts think that the accounting profession is one of the fastest routes to the top of a corporation.

According to a government forecast, the demand for accountants and auditors will increase 10 to 20 percent through 2012. As the economy grows, the number of business establishments will increase, requiring more accountants and auditors to set up books, prepare taxes, and provide management advice. As these businesses grow, the volume and complexity of information developed by accountants and auditors regarding costs, expenditures, and taxes will increase as well. Increased need for accountants and auditors will arise from changes in legislation related to taxes, financial reporting standards, business investments, mergers, and other financial matters. The growth of international business also has led to more demand for accounting expertise and services related to international trade and accounting rules, as well as to international mergers and acquisitions. These trends should create more jobs for accountants and auditors.

As a result of recent accounting scandals, federal legislation was enacted to increase penalties and make company executives personally responsible for falsely reporting financial information. These changes should lead to increased scrutiny of company finances and accounting procedures and should create opportunities for accountants and auditors, particularly CPAs, to more thoroughly audit financial records. In order to ensure that finances comply with the law before public accountants conduct audits, management accountants and internal auditors will increasingly be needed to discover and eliminate fraud. The demand for government accountants should increase in response to the effort to make government agencies more efficient and accountable.

Increased awareness of financial crimes such as embezzlement, bribery, and securities fraud will also increase the demand for forensic accountants to detect illegal financial activity by individuals, companies, and organized crime rings. Computer technology has made these crimes easier to commit, and they are on the rise. But development of new computer software and electronic surveillance technology has also made tracking down financial criminals easier, thus increasing the ease and likelihood that forensic accountants will discover their crimes. As success rates of investigations grow, demand for forensic accountants will also grow.

The changing role of accountants and auditors also will spur job growth, although this growth will be limited as a result of financial scandals. In response to demand, some accountants are offering more financial management and consulting services as they assume a greater advisory role and develop more sophisticated accounting systems. Since federal legislation now prohibits accountants from providing nontraditional services to clients whose books they audit, opportunities for accountants to do non-audit work could be limited. However, accountants will still be able to advise on other financial matters for clients that are not publicly traded companies and for non-audit clients, but growth in these areas will be slower than in the past. Also, due to the increasing popularity of tax preparation firms and computer software, accountants will shift away from tax preparation. As computer programs continue to simplify some accounting-related tasks, clerical staff will increasingly handle many routine calculations.

Overall, job opportunities for accountants and auditors should be favorable. After most states instituted the 150-hour rule for CPAs, enrollment in accounting programs declined; however, enrollment is slowly beginning to grow again as more students are attracted to the profession because of the attention from the accounting scandals. Those who pursue a CPA should have excellent job prospects. In addition, many accounting graduates are pursuing other certifications such as the CMA and CIA, so competition could be greater in management accounting and internal auditing than in public accounting. Regardless of specialty, accountants and auditors who have earned professional recognition through certification or licensure should have the best job prospects. Applicants with a master's degree in accounting, or a master's degree in business administration with a concentration in accounting, also will have an advantage. In the aftermath of the accounting scandals, professional certification is even more important to ensure that the accountants' credentials and ethics are sound.

SUGGESTED READING

Publications are available from the various organizations that offer certification and licensing. Also of interest is the annual *Salary Guide for Accounting, Finance, and Information Technology* from Robert Half International, Inc.

CHAPTER 3

OPPORTUNITIES WITH GOVERNMENT

The federal government is the largest single employer in the United States, with employees stationed in all parts of the nation and in many foreign countries. Over one million people are employed by the federal government's executive branch.

State and local governments are also large employers. There are 50 state governments and 87,525 local governments employing tens of millions of people. Approximately one of every five employed civilians works in a government position.

Governments experienced rapid growth in the 1980s, which led to an increase in the number of positions for government accountants. According to the Bureau of Labor Statistics, over 215,000 accountants work for municipal, county, state, and federal governments. In 2002, more than 34,000 accountants and auditors worked for the federal government, earning an average annual salary of $63,370.

Newspapers across the nation abound with such reports as "State auditor finds shortage in City of X general fund bank account" and "County Y ended the year with a cash balance of $350,000, but unrecorded carryover bills would have resulted in a deficit of $500,000."

Skilled trained accountants are in great demand in all areas of government. The government hires accountants for regular accounting positions and as auditors. Government accountants examine records of government agencies, businesses, and individuals. Accountants with the federal government may work as Internal Revenue Service agents, investigators, and bank examiners.

If one wants to be an accountant, why work for the government? Read the following words of three accountants who chose the government career track to see whether this might be the place for you.

My parents were foreign-born. I had no opportunity to attend college, but I was very good at math and quick to learn. So I took a civil service test, passed it, and started out as an accounting technician. True, it was the lowest level at which one could start, but I accepted on-the-job training and have been promoted several grade levels. The government is an equal opportunity employer.

A Vietnam veteran with several years of college accounting courses says,

Veterans receive preference on civil service positions, and I wanted the stability, salary, and pension that go with government employment.

A college graduate who majored in accounting gives this reason for choosing to work for the government:

My brother, an FBI agent, told me the Internal Revenue Service needed good, inquisitive people. I like working with taxes and with people, and I love to travel. I am very happy as an Internal Revenue Service agent and plan to make a career of it.

FEDERAL GOVERNMENT CAREERS

The U.S. federal government is divided into three branches: legislative, executive, and judicial. The legislative branch levies taxes and authorizes expenditures through a budget. The executive branch prepares the budget and carries out the programs. The judicial branch interprets the laws. Accounting functions for the federal government are the responsibility of the executive and legislative branches. Accountants are typically employed within the following areas:

Executive Branch

Office of Management and Budget (OMB): prepares federal budget, makes appropriations

Department of the Treasury: handles cash receipts and disbursements

Central Accounting: manages public debt

General Services Administration: handles financial management

Federal agencies (departments): accountants manage agency resources, maintain agency accounting systems, prepare agency budgets and reports

Legislative Branch

Government Accountability Office (GAO): audits, investigates, and evaluates programs, activities, and financial operations of federal departments and agencies; prescribes accounting standards; approves agency accounting systems; makes special investigations

About 90 percent of federal employees are covered by a merit system and most of these functions are handled by the Office of Personnel Management. Most states have merit systems patterned after that of the federal government. Federal positions are classified according to eighteen grade (levels) which make up the General Schedule and are referred to as GS grades (see Table 3.1). This grade pay schedule usually is updated in October of each year. The GS rating is based on the quality and extent of education and experience.

The lower grade levels, GS-1 through GS-4, include clerical and technical positions. Grades GS-5 through GS-11 are comparable to lower middle management in industry. Grade level GS-5 has a salary similar to those offered new college graduates by private companies. A GS-5 employee, after one year, has a good opportunity for promotion. The most common entry-level grades for college graduates are GS-5, GS-7, GS-9, and GS-11. Each accounting job description will designate the grade level for that position. Within each grade are pay steps that show the range of compensation possible for competent job performance.

Promotions from one grade to the next are not guaranteed, but many are granted at one- to three-year intervals. The federal government believes that the salaries of its employees should be comparable to those paid by

Table 3.1 General Schedule of Annual Salary Rates

ANNUAL RATES BY GRADE AND STEP

GS Grade	Step 1	Step 2	Step 3	Step 4	Step 5	Step 6	Step 7	Step 8	Step 9	Step 10
GS-1	$16,016	$16,550	$17,083	$17,613	$18,146	$18,459	$18,984	$19,515	$19,537	$20,036
GS-2	18,007	18,435	19,031	19,537	19,755	20,336	20,917	21,498	22,079	22,660
GS-3	19,647	20,302	20,957	21,612	22,267	22,922	23,577	24,232	24,887	25,542
GS-4	22,056	22,791	23,526	24,261	24,996	25,731	26,466	27,201	27,936	28,671
GS-5	24,677	25,500	26,323	27,146	27,969	28,792	29,615	30,438	31,261	32,084
GS-6	27,507	28,424	29,341	30,258	31,175	32,092	33,009	33,926	34,843	35,760
GS-7	30,567	31,586	32,605	33,624	34,643	35,662	36,681	37,700	38,719	39,738
GS-8	33,852	34,980	36,108	37,236	38,364	39,492	40,620	41,748	42,876	44,004
GS-9	37,390	38,636	39,882	41,128	42,374	43,620	44,866	46,112	47,358	48,604
GS-10	41,175	42,548	43,921	45,294	46,667	48,040	49,413	50,786	52,159	53,532
GS-11	45,239	46,747	48,255	49,763	51,271	52,779	54,287	55,795	57,303	58,811
GS-12	54,221	56,028	57,835	59,642	61,449	63,256	65,063	66,870	68,677	70,484
GS-13	64,478	66,627	68,776	70,925	73,074	75,223	77,372	79,521	81,670	83,819
GS-14	76,193	78,733	81,273	83,813	86,353	88,893	91,433	93,973	96,513	99,053
GS-15	89,625	92,613	95,601	98,589	101,577	104,565	107,553	110,541	113,529	116,517

Source: U.S. Office of Personnel Management, Washington, D.C., 2005. General Schedule Incorporating a 2.50 percent General Schedule Increase.

Note: Pay schedules are adjusted for cost of living by locality. Those adjustments are not shown here. Check locality tables for exact rates.

private employers for the same level of work and believes in the principle "equal pay for equal work." A general practice is to promote from within.

Government accountants perform a variety of duties, including:

- Preparing the nation's budget
- Auditing public utilities
- Reviewing financial conditions of banks
- Studying the background of bankruptcies
- Examining the books of stock exchange firms
- Reviewing amounts spent by the various government agencies

The following occupations are open to accountants interested in careers with the federal government.

Accounting Technician

The accounting technician, or bookkeeper, performs a variety of routine duties including keeping journals and ledgers, preparing the payroll, writing cash reports, and updating accounting forms. The technician may use office equipment such as calculators and computers. Advancement within the same grade level may be to more responsible assignments such as preparing financial statements.

Positions for accounting technicians generally start at the GS-5 level; salary is dependent on education and experience. For starting levels higher than GS-5, applicants must have one year of specialized experience equivalent to the next lower grade level.

Accountant

The duties of the accountant are:

- To collect and evaluate accounting data
- To maintain accounting records
- To establish and revise accounting systems
- To prepare and analyze financial statements
- To safeguard and maintain control over assets
- To maintain cost systems
- To incorporate a budget into the system
- To comply with all federal regulations

Education and diversity of experience will determine the GS rating at which the accountant will enter government service.

GS-5. To enter at the GS-5 level, an applicant normally meets one of the following requirements:
- Four years of accounting in college
- Three years' accounting experience
- An equivalent combination of education and experience
- A CPA certificate

GS-7. An applicant can enter at the GS-7 level by meeting the GS-5 requirement plus one year of graduate study in accounting or one additional year's experience in accounting. The civil service examination must be taken if the experience requirements are not met. The examination need not be taken if the applicant meets the educational or certification requirement.

GS-9. A college graduate with an accounting major or a holder of a CPA certificate qualifies for grades GS-9, GS-11, and GS-12 without taking a written test. Accounting experience of three to five years is required for grade GS-9, and three to six years of experience is required for grades GS-11 through GS-15. Applicants eligible for grades GS-13 and above are exempt from a written test. All others must either take the written test in accounting or meet the experience and education requirements. Refer to Table 3.2 for salary structure. Check with the OPM for the latest requirements (usajobs.gov).

Auditor

The government auditor investigates the accounting records of government units and agencies and renders an opinion to interested users, primarily the federal government.

The federal government requires audits of its grant programs to ensure that the funds are used as specified in the grant. Underwriting and rating agencies ask for audited financial statements from a city that wishes to issue bonds. State and local governmental units that receive certain amounts of federal financial assistance are required to have an independent audit of

Table 3.2   Securities and Exchange Commission Accountant Special Salary Rates

ANNUAL RATES BY GRADE AND STEP

GS level	52 weeks			104 weeks			156 weeks			
	1	2	3	4	5	6	7	8	9	10
GS-12	$47,180	$48,610	$50,040	$51,470	$52,900	$54,330	$55,760	$57,190	$58,620	$60,050
GS-13	56,103	57,803	59,503	61,203	62,903	64,603	66,303	68,003	69,703	71,403
GS-14	66,297	68,306	70,315	72,324	74,333	76,342	78,351	80,360	82,369	84,378
GS-15	77,983	80,346	82,709	85,072	87,435	89,798	92,161	94,524	96,887	99,250

Source: SEC, Washington, D.C. Check locality tables for Boston, Chicago, Los Angeles, New York, San Francisco. Exact salaries differ from locality to locality.

funds obtained under such programs. Consequently, governmental auditing has become both a professional and a personal challenge. The need for governmental auditors will continue well into the next decade.

Successful auditors possess certain personal qualifications. The auditor must have an analytical mind and be knowledgeable about government accounting principles and methodology. The individual should be able to communicate clearly through oral and written reports. Additional qualities include the ability to handle responsibility, to work with little supervision, and to concentrate on details without overlooking long-range goals. Mental flexibility to quickly absorb facts and make judgments and to work with systems and computers is necessary. The auditor must be persuasive and tactful in dealing with people.

Because the auditing field is growing so rapidly, auditors find advancement opportunities early in their careers. Auditors are encouraged to take on more responsible work, which, in turn, qualifies them for promotion to higher grades and higher salary levels. The government offers training programs to help the employee prepare for advancement. A beginning auditor can advance in two to three years. New jobs are created by government legislation, conservation, and pollution. The auditor will conduct reviews of businesses for compliance with the prescribed regulations. A college degree will be required for the future. An auditor may become certified through a test administered by the Institute of Internal Auditors. Certification affirms competence and professional status. (The process of becoming certified is discussed in Chapter 2.)

The 2003 revision of Government Auditing Standards (known as the "Yellow Book") stipulates specific continuing education requirements for individuals who work on "audits of government organizations, programs, activities and functions." Auditors responsible for "planning, directing, conducting or reporting on government audits" are required to complete eighty hours of continuing education every two years. At least twenty-four of these hours should be in subjects "directly related to the government environment and to government auditing."

Typical audit procedures are applied to evaluate the system of internal control and to test and review the account balances.

Government audits fall into two main categories:

- Financial and compliance audits
- Performance audits; economy, efficiency, and program results audits

Financial and compliance audits determine whether the financial statements fairly present the financial position and results of operations of the government unit or agency in accordance with generally accepted accounting principles, and whether the entity has complied with applicable federal laws and regulations. The financial and compliance audit is very similar to an audit rendered by a public accounting firm for an industrial corporation.

An economy and efficiency audit will determine whether the government unit is managing its assets, primarily its people and property, in an economic and efficient manner.

A program results audit determines the fair presentation of the results of various government programs.

Other types of audits help legislative committees during congressional hearings or forecast outcomes of programs. Government accountants sometimes are directed to do highly sensitive investigative work, too.

Auditors are employed by the federal government at the same levels as accountants. Educational and experience requirements and pay scales are the same as those previously discussed for the GS-5, GS-7, GS-9, and GS-11 through GS-15 grades.

Defense Contract Auditor

The Defense Contract Audit Agency (DCAA) provides standardized contract audit services for the Department of Defense, as well as accounting and financial advisory services regarding contracts and subcontracts to all Department of Defense components responsible for procurement and contract administration. These services are provided in connection with negotiation, administration, and settlement of contracts and subcontracts. DCAA also provides contract audit services to some other government agencies. The DCAA employs approximately four thousand people located at more than three hundred field audit offices throughout the United States, Europe, and in the Pacific.

Candidates for DCAA must be American citizens who have or will complete a minimum of twenty-four semester hours in accounting or auditing (up to six semester hours of which may be in business law) as part of successful completion of a four-year academic course of study.

Newly hired auditors receive over three hundred hours of continuing professional education training during their first two years, and an average of sixty hours per year thereafter. This specialized training is provided through the DCAA Institute located in Memphis, Tennessee.

In addition to training, DCAA supports attainment of professional certifications and advanced degrees (for example, CPA, CIA, M.B.A., M.P.A.) by its auditors. The agency sponsors CPA coaching courses and pays for courses taken in pursuit of advanced degrees. Salaries are based on the GS wage scale.

Internal Revenue Service Agent

The Internal Revenue Service (IRS) agent examines and audits the accounting books and records of individuals, partnerships, fiduciaries, and corporations to determine their correct federal tax liability. An agent may specialize in one area, such as dealing exclusively with individuals or only with corporations. The IRS audits every kind of business and, therefore, offers an auditor a high degree of client diversity.

An applicant for this position must meet one of the following requirements: fours years of college with an accounting major; three years' experience comparable to four years of college; any equivalent combination of education and experience; or a CPA certificate. The individual with a college education is rated on his or her academic achievement and the quality and variety of experience. An applicant with experience only must take the written civil service test.

Promotions tend to be based on merit. If the accountant does not wish to travel, positions are available that involve less travel. Often an accountant who has retired from service with the IRS finds tax season employment with the smaller public accounting firms.

An entry position for an Internal Revenue Service agent is at GS-5 or GS-7. The applicant with a college degree in accounting will enter at the higher level.

Revenue Officer

A revenue officer collects delinquent taxes, investigates business situations, negotiates agreements to satisfy tax obligations, and performs other tasks to safeguard the government's interests. The revenue officer is essentially a tax collector.

A written civil service exam must be taken and the revenue officer enters government employment at either the GS-5 or GS-7 level.

Securities Investigator

A securities investigator will examine the books, records, and financial statements of national securities exchanges, over-the-counter brokers, and investment advisers to determine their financial condition and compliance with the law. Fraud cases are investigated.

The applicant must have accounting, auditing, investigative, or administrative experience in the securities field. Education may be substituted for experience. No written test is required. Grade GS-9 requires three to five years' experience and grade GS-11 requires three to six years. Starting salaries for grades GS-9 and GS-11 are in Table 3.1. The applicant's GS rating is based on the quality and extent of experience and training.

Special Agent, Internal Revenue Service

A special agent with the Internal Revenue Service conducts investigations of alleged criminal violations of the federal tax laws, makes recommendations with respect to prosecution, prepares technical reports, and assists a U.S. attorney in the preparation of a case and trial.

All of the IRS's special agents are accountants. Special agents enjoy a great deal of flexibility in their work and may find it extremely satisfying if they like law enforcement combined with accounting.

The work of a special agent may involve a single tax avoidance case, a money laundering investigation, or a complex investigation into drug trafficking. In recent years special agents have served as financial experts in the Federal Organized Crime Strike Force Program and the Organized Crime Drug Enforcement Task Force.

The applicant must have three years' experience and a knowledge of accounting and auditing, or four years of college, including twelve semester hours in accounting, or a law degree. The rating is based on the results of a written test. The entry-level position is at GS-5 or GS-7 level.

Special Agent, Federal Bureau of Investigation

The FBI is interested in seeking certified public accountants as special agents. Applicants must be U.S. citizens, between the ages of twenty-three and thirty-five, in excellent physical health, and available for transfer anywhere in the United States. Special agents with law and accounting backgrounds are being sought primarily for the FBI's continuing battle with white-collar and organized crime. Typical assignments of CPA agents might include tracing the flow of funds used to finance narcotics operations; examining political corruption; investigating contamination of consumer products, bank robbery, kidnapping, and extortion.

All special agents are trained at the New Agent's Training School near Quantico, Virginia. The training consists of a rigorous fifteen-week course in FBI rules and regulations, investigative techniques, and criminal court procedure. Agents must also become proficient in the use of firearms and defensive tactics.

Applicants undergo a written examination followed by a personal interview and an extensive background check that can take up to six months to complete. Successful applicants begin employment at the GS-10 level, serve a one-year probationary period, and then become a permanent employee upon satisfactorily completing the trial period.

For information, visit the agency's website at fbi.gov.

Tax Technician, Internal Revenue Service

The tax technician represents the IRS when consulting with taxpayers to identify and explain tax issues and to determine correct tax liabilities.

All applicants must pass a written examination. College graduates should have a combined total of twenty-four semester hours in accounting, business administration, finance, and economics. The tax technician enters government employment at the GS-5 or GS-7 grade level. A government worker with a master's degree or two years' experience starts at the GS-9 level.

In addition to the central accounting office of the federal government, certain specialized departments that hire many accountants and deserve separate mention are the General Accounting Office, the federal agencies (departments), and the Securities and Exchange Commission.

Government Accountability Office (GAO) Accountant or Auditor

The Government Accountability Office (GAO) is the congressional watchdog over executive agencies and the internal audit department of the U.S. government. The department, originally called the General Accounting Office, was renamed in July 2004 to better reflect the full scope of modern professional services offered by the GAO. The GAO employs over 3,500 individuals. Many GAO employees are accountants and auditors, and more than half work in Washington, D.C. These accountants and auditors, hired at the GS levels already explained, review programs of the various federal agencies to ensure against duplication and to evaluate the cost, efficiency, and success of these programs. In addition to audits, they settle claims against the government and collect debts.

Financial auditors must have an undergraduate or graduate degree that includes twenty-four semester hours, or equivalent, of coursework in accounting and related subjects; other requirements also apply. Entry financial auditors are assigned to GAO's Professional Development Program in the Financial Management and Assurance Team. The U.S. General Accountability Office is headquartered at 441 G Street NW, Washington, DC 20548, with eleven regional offices throughout the United States. Complete information is available at the website, gao.gov.

Only part of the responsibilities of a GAO auditor relate to financial auditing. Auditors spend much of their time evaluating the management of federal programs and assessing their effectiveness in meeting program goals.

The major organizational units of the GAO that specifically use the services of accountants and auditors are:

- **Policy and Program Planning.** Oversees that audit work of the GAO is planned, coordinated, and reported.
- **Accounting and Financial Management Division.** Coordinates automatic data processing, internal auditing, accounting and financial reporting, fraud prevention, and financial statement audits.
- **Energy and Minerals Division.** Provides audit coverage for the Department of Energy, the Nuclear Regulatory Commission, and similar agencies.
- **Federal Personnel and Compensation Division.** Provides audit coverage for the Office of Personnel Management, Selective Service System, and others.
- **Field Operations Division.** Conducts audits throughout the United States, Puerto Rico, and the Virgin Islands. About half the GAO's professional staff is assigned to the regional offices, located in Atlanta, Boston, Chicago, Dallas, Dayton, Denver, Huntsville, Los Angeles, Norfolk, San Francisco, and Seattle.

- **General Government Division.** Provides audit coverage for the Departments of Justice and the Treasury, the District of Columbia government, the U.S. Postal Service, the judicial branch of the federal government, plus various agencies and commissions.
- **International Division.** Provides audit coverage for the Department of State, the Central Intelligence Agency, the Export-Import Bank, the Office of U.S. Trade, the International Trade Commission, and other organizations.

The GAO offers a computerized employment application processing system, GAO Careers, which electronically prescreens candidates and ranks them according to specified criteria. GAO Careers lets you browse for available jobs in GAO; create, edit, and archive your electronic résumé; and apply for specific jobs online. GAO Careers also allows you to identify the type(s) of jobs you are interested in, and will then notify you with an e-mail message when that kind of job is open for application.

Agency Auditor

Besides the GAO, federal auditors work for various departments and agencies:

- Department of Health and Human Services
- Farm Credit Administration
- Department of Defense
- Department of Agriculture
- Air Force Audit Agency
- Army Audit Agency
- Defense Contract Audit Agency
- Navy Audit Agency
- Department of the Interior
- Federal Power Commission
- Federal Highway Administration
- Interstate Commerce Commission

Each department and agency has a small staff of accountants and auditors, who are hired at entry-level positions. These federal accountants and auditors evaluate the policies, systems, procedures, records, and reports. They audit contracts with establishments engaged in defense and space work, concessionaires in the national park system, and public utilities, as well as the government's royalties from production of leased minerals and the reports of interstate carriers filed with the Interstate Commerce Commission.

Securities and Exchange Commission (SEC) Accountant

The SEC employs accountants in the following divisions: the Division of Corporation Finance, Division of Enforcement, and the Office of the Chief Accountant, all located in Washington, D.C. Limited opportunities are also available in the Division of Market Regulation, Division of Investment Management, and the Office of Compliance, Inspections and Examinations and in the SEC's eleven regional and district offices nationwide. These offices are located in Atlanta, Boston, Chicago, Denver, Fort Worth, Los Angeles, Miami, New York, Philadelphia, Salt Lake City, and San Francisco. SEC divisions and offices offer accountants a wide variety of work, such as examining financial statements in public filings, finding solutions to the most difficult and controversial accounting issues, and rule-writing opportunities.

The main responsibilities of accountants in the Division of Corporate Finance are as follows:

- Review financial statements and disclosures for a variety of complex transactions, as well as interesting and unusual accounting, auditing, and factual issues
- Review filings to identify potential or actual material accounting, auditing, financial reporting, or disclosure deficiencies resulting from deviations from GAAP, GAAS, or the accounting rules and policies of the SEC
- Interact with top professionals in the accounting and securities industries
- Influence accounting standards and practices
- Propose new and amended disclosure rules
- Field questions from registrants, prospective registrants, and the public

The Division of Enforcement monitors the U.S. securities markets and its participants, including public companies and their auditors. In this capacity, auditors are responsible for the following functions:

- Participate in defining the scope of financial fraud investigations
- Analyze and assess data obtained in the course of investigations
- Advise the legal staff of relevant accounting and auditing standards
- Participate in interviews and depositions and litigation matters
- Cooperate with criminal investigators, as necessary

The SEC typically hires experienced accountants into mid- and senior staff accountant positions at the SK-13 through 17 levels. The most desirable candidates are CPAs with three to eight years of public accounting experience related to the securities industry. This may include audit work involving SEC financial reporting; complex internal audit work involving multinational corporations; or mergers and acquisitions related work. Grade determinations are made based on amount of relevant work experience and/or graduate education in accounting, finance, or related fields. Specific requirements are explained in each posting.

The SEC has a special pay schedule comparable to the federal banking regulators. Employees receive pay plus a locality percentage based on their office location. Individual salary levels are determined based on qualifications, previous accounting experience, and salary history. Depending on the office and position, in 2005 most experienced accountants are hired at SK-13 (approximately $91,000 to $119,000) or SK-14 (approximately $106,000 to $136,000). Some experienced accountants may also be hired into the nonsupervisory SK-16 (approximately $121,000 to $155,000). Finally, supervisors may be hired or promoted into SK-15 (approximately $109,000 to $139,000) and SK-17 (approximately $129,000 to $165,000) at the SEC. The SEC rewards superior performance with advancement to a higher step within the current grade, awards, and/or promotions to the next grade level.

SEC national headquarters are located at 100 F Street NE, Washington, DC 20549. The agency maintains regional offices in New York, Boston, Philadelphia, Miami, Atlanta, Chicago, Denver, Fort Worth, Salt Lake City, Los Angeles, and San Francisco. Mailing addresses of the district offices are available at the agency's website, sec.gov.

Summer Employment for Students

The Office of Personnel Management (OPM) offers summer employment and various temporary positions for students. Summer positions are detailed in Announcement 414, "Summer Jobs," which is issued by the OPM in autumn every year. Summer months worked will count toward total years of service if permanent employment is later taken with the federal government. Anticipated openings for the following summer are listed in the announcement. Summer and temporary positions are detailed at the website, studentjobs.gov.

Salary Progression

Many agencies hire accountants and auditors at the GS-7 level. Promotion goes to GS-9, GS-11, and GS-12 levels. Excellent performance can lead to a pay increase of almost 80 percent in three years. Accountants working in areas where supply is limited may receive a higher starting salary. In 1989, the GAO implemented a "pay for performance" system in which annual bonuses were awarded to the top 50 percent of the staff.

How quickly an employee is promoted depends upon openings available in the higher grades and upon the employee's ability. Federal employees receive on-the-job training and participate in career development programs. An employee's performance is evaluated and rated annually. Competition for the higher positions is keen. Only the most qualified rise to the higher grade levels where fewer positions are available. A disadvantage of government service is lack of competitive salary at the higher grade levels. Higher grade positions with the government usually command a lower salary than the employee could obtain with a job in private industry.

Work Force Reductions

Federal government layoffs are called reductions in force. These reductions may be caused by a decrease in work or a cut in appropriations. Whether an employee is retained depends upon security, job performance, veteran preference, and whether the appointment is career, conditional, or temporary. Employees are entitled to unemployment compensation if they are laid off.

Time Off

Government employment has a number of benefits. Federal employees earn thirteen days of vacation leave a year for the first three years and twenty days a year for the next twelve years. After fifteen years they are entitled to twenty-six days of leave each year. Paid holidays are New Year's Day, Martin Luther King Jr.'s Birthday, President's Day, Memorial Day, Independence Day, Columbus Day, Veteran's Day, Thanksgiving, and Christmas.

Employees are entitled to thirteen days per year sick leave, which may be used for illness and medical appointments. Unused sick leave may accumulate for future use.

Many agencies have adopted a flexible work schedule that permits employees to work their biweekly eighty hours in fewer days by working nine- to ten-hour days. This allows individuals to arrange their work schedules to fit personal needs.

Child Care

In response to the needs of working couples and single parents for convenient child care centers, many federal agencies now provide such centers. The GAO also offers child care centers.

Insurance Programs

Employees have the usual fringe benefits of life insurance, medical insurance, and retirement pension. The health insurance program offers a choice of plans and provides immediate coverage from the date of enrollment. The life insurance is a basic policy based upon salary and includes three options to increase the amount of coverage and include family members.

Retirement Benefits

The retirement plan provides employees with several options and is portable. Portability enables a person to leave government service after a minimum number of years and still qualify for benefits.

The retirement program consists of three parts: Social Security benefits, a basic benefit plan, and a savings plan. For the savings plan, employees may contribute up to 10 percent of their pay, and the government will contribute up to 5 percent. The savings may be invested in a government securities fund, a fixed income fund, or a common stock index fund.

STATE GOVERNMENT CAREERS

Within state government, accountants are employed by the department of audit and control and the department of taxation and finance. Beginning positions are junior accountant, junior auditor, and tax examiner, with promotion to assistant accountant, assistant auditor, senior income tax examiner, and senior commodities tax examiner.

Junior Accountant/Auditor

The junior accountant or auditor works in a state agency whose records are subject to review. Some of the duties of the accountant are to maintain accounting records, supervise clerks who journalize and post, maintain a general ledger, and prepare financial statements.

An auditor, for example, may examine the records of state and local agencies for accuracy and legality, reconcile bank statements, verify financial statements, and review payroll. Prior to the mid-1970s, the auditor was a technician. Today, he or she is a professional who understands government, law, public finances, and computers, and adheres to standards of professional performance. State auditors perform financial and compliance audits for many state and local governments.

Both the accountant and the auditor work under supervision. Requirements for these positions are four years of college with twenty-four semester hours in accounting or an equivalent combination of education and experience. In addition to knowledge of accounting, accountants and auditors need to work well with people, to understand instructions, and to be accurate and neat.

Tax Examiner

Under supervision, the tax examiner audits tax returns of individuals and businesses either in the office or in the field. The examiner working within the department of tax and finance specializes in one of the following areas: commodities tax, corporate tax, state income tax, state sales tax, or state franchise tax. The commodities tax bureau employs examiners to check the accounting records and inventories of distributors of alcoholic beverages, motor fuels, cigarettes, and so forth. Examiners working in the corporate tax bureau perform such duties as field audits of corporations, verification of corporate tax reports, location of delinquent corporations, and examination of bankruptcies. A tax examiner with a state income tax bureau examines individual tax returns, reviews questionable items, and approves assessments and refunds. For all positions as tax examiner, a college degree with an accounting major or an equivalent combination of education and experience is required. Qualifications are the same as for accountant or auditor.

Employment Opportunities and Salaries

Salary information and employment opportunities may be obtained by contacting a state's civil service commission, employment bureaus, and other appropiate agencies. Most state government positions require that the applicant pass written and oral examinations similar to those required for civil service positions with the federal government.

Salaries of state government employees vary widely. Geographic location of the state and the size of the population can make a considerable difference in salaries. A large, densely populated state such as California may pay more than a smaller state. According to the Bureau of Labor Statistics, in 2002 accountants and auditors employed by state governments earned an average annual salary of $42,680.

CITY AND LOCAL GOVERNMENT CAREERS

Most municipalities, counties, and townships of any size are required to keep records in accordance with standards and guidelines established for government units. In addition to state governments, thousands of local governments are required to have an annual financial and compliance audit. An audit opinion is rendered.

Cities that are required to undergo an annual audit, and many others as well, hire college graduates with degrees in accounting. They must maintain their records in conformity with state regulations and with recommended government accounting principles and procedures.

A typical city of five hundred thousand people may have three accounting positions: accountant, staff accountant, and accounts administrator, in ascending order.

Accountant

Working under general supervision, the accountant performs moderately difficult work in the classification, analysis, and reporting of financial data. Technical supervision may be provided for clerical personnel.

Duties of the accountant include maintaining books of original entry and subsidiary ledgers; preparation of journal entries, postings, trial balances, and reports; and periodic examination of receipts, warrants, purchases, vouchers, payroll records, and billings to ascertain that transactions and documents are prepared according to established procedures. The accountant ensures that internal checks and balances are operating efficiently; makes recommendations for modifications in accounting and office forms and procedures; and audits cash receipts, ledgers, journals, and inventories.

The accountant must possess a broad knowledge of government accounting principles, practices, and procedures; auditing; electronic, financial, and accounting systems; business administration procedures; and general office procedures.

Educational requirements are graduation from an accredited college with a bachelor's degree in business administration with a major in accounting, and one year of professional accounting experience.

Staff Accountant

The staff accountant supervises accounting work that involves major accounting and fiscal operations. He or she also develops and installs accounting systems and controls. Examples of the duties performed are:

- Application of accounting principles to install, develop, and maintain the accounting system
- Supervision of accounting work for a particular accounting function of considerable size and complexity
- Supervision of the installation of accounting controls
- Setting up ledgers, journals, and reporting procedures
- Assigning account codes and classifications to transactions
- Implementing changes to improve efficiency or control
- Preparing detailed financial analyses of projects, proposals, and federal reports
- Providing accounting information and financial advice to the administrative staff as requested

Considerable knowledge is required of accounting principles, practices, and procedures; of government accounting; of electronic, financial, and accounting information systems; and of business administration procedures. Supervisory skills in handling personnel are needed. Skill in analyzing financial data, in developing and installing accounting systems and controls, and in preparing reports is necessary.

Educational requirements are a bachelor's degree in accounting from an accredited college or university and four years of professional accounting experience. A master's degree in arts or business administration and one year of professional accounting experience may be accepted in lieu of the four years of professional accounting experience.

Accounts Administrator

The accounts administrator provides professional assistance and guidance to the accounting personnel in the areas of accounts payable, accounts receivable, budget control, payroll, and data entry. He or she also resolves special projects and problems.

The accounts administrator supervises the following systems: accounts payable system, vouchers systems, accounts receivable system, budgeting, payroll, and data entry in the electronic data processing system. The administrator also bears the responsibility for overseeing the general administrative duties for the division. In addition, the administrator prepares cost distribution reports, provides assistance to other departments regarding accounting-related problems, and prepares a variety of complex reports and analyses.

Considerable knowledge of automated accounting systems and of business administration procedures is required. Skills are needed in office procedures and techniques, in supervising personnel, in identifying and analyzing problems and resolving them, and in oral and written communication.

A bachelor's degree in accounting from an accredited college or university plus five years of accounting experience are required. A master's degree in business administration and two years of professional accounting may be accepted in lieu of the five years of professional accounting experience.

In a typical city of five hundred thousand inhabitants, all three municipal accounting positions would be under the municipal civil service commission, which is usually similar to the federal system. Cities have their own civil service examination which conforms to the requirements of the accounting positions required by the municipality.

Salaries of city and local government employees vary according to the geographic locality and population of the government unit involved. The Bureau of Labor Statistics reports that in 2002, accountants employed by local governments earned an average annual salary of $44,690. Salaries vary according to level of responsibility, education, and experience. Employees work a forty-hour week and are covered by a retirement system. They are entitled to sick pay and vacation pay. Salary information and employment opportunities may be obtained by contacting the appropriate local civil service commission.

CIVIL SERVICE (OFFICE OF PERSONNEL MANAGEMENT)

Civil service is the name given to the government departments that are not part of the military service. Civil service includes most nonelective, non-policy-making positions for the federal, state, county, or city governments. Employment positions and promotions are obtained through a system of competitive examinations, called the merit system. Under the merit system an individual must prove he or she is qualified for employment in the government service. Civil service was established in 1883 when Congress passed the Pendleton Act. Civil service replaced the spoils system, which rewarded individuals with government jobs as payment for favors done for a political party.

The federal government alone has approximately one hundred agencies. State and local governments have many more. Each of the different agencies has positions with similar duties. These positions are grouped into one classification for which an examination may be given. Thus, a person applying for staff accountant for a Department of Agriculture agency will take the same exam as one applying for staff accountant with the Department of Health and Human Services.

In 1979, the Civil Service Commission was abolished; its functions have since been handled by the Office of Personnel Management (OPM). The OPM is based in Washington, D.C., and has area offices throughout the United States. Your local area office will be listed in the telephone book under "United States Government." These offices maintain a Federal

Employment Service Center which will have information about current positions available, overseas employment, job requirements and qualifications, and examination procedures. At the end of this chapter is a list of the Federal Employment Service Centers in the United States.

Job opportunities with a state government can be determined by contacting the nearest state employment service office. Or it is possible to write the state civil service commission in the capital city of the state. Many large cities will have a civil service commission. Other sources of information are the municipal building and the public library.

USAJOBS

The federal government maintains a website that details over 18,800 available jobs worldwide. USAJOBS (usajobs.gov) allows users to search for jobs and create résumés. Job listings include complete details about duties, qualifications, benefits, and the application procedure.

New users to the site are encouraged to follow three steps to find a job.

1. Create an account. This allows users to create and post résumés and to receive e-mail notifications of jobs.
2. Search for jobs. Enter your search criteria and use your posted résumé to apply for jobs instantly.
3. Manage your career. This part of the site allows users to match jobs to their interests, find specific jobs, and match federal jobs to positions in the private sector.

USAJOBS also provides tutorials and guides to help job seekers conduct a successful search. The site also lists educational opportunities provided by the federal government, including apprenticeships, grants, internships, scholarships, and cooperative opportunities.

Application Procedure

Applications for federal positions can be made by submitting a résumé, an Optional Application for Federal Employment form (OF 612), or by another written format. The OF 612 form generally includes all of the information that will be required for submitting an application. If your résumé or letter of application does not include all required information, you might not be considered for the job. Basically, you must provide your personal information (address and contact information), work experience, education, and other qualifications. Be sure to complete the form carefully and thoroughly.

The federal government accepts applications for posted positions by internet and postal mail. To apply online, visit usajobs.gov. When you have located the position(s) in which you are interested, click on the "how to apply" tab, then use the link to "apply online" at the bottom of the page. Be sure to read the entire job announcement to determine which documentation and forms you will need to complete your application. You will need to establish a user account in order to apply online.

If you prefer to apply by postal mail, you can send all required paperwork to the mailing address listed in each job announcement.

Written Test

If a test is required for the position, you will be notified as to when and where to report for the test. Applicants are advised to go to the public library and obtain the most current book on how to study and prepare for the civil service test. Study the material and become proficient on the subjects that will be covered. On competitive exams, all applicants compete with one another. The higher your examination grade, the better your chance of being appointed. There are no fees charged to take any of the tests, and the tests may be retaken, although some are given infrequently. If you pass the test with a grade of 70 or higher, your name will be placed on a list from which appointments are made.

Veterans' Preference

Ten extra points will be added to the applicant's test score if he or she is a disabled veteran or the wife of one, a widow of certain veterans, or a widowed or divorced mother of a veteran who died in service or of one who is totally and permanently disabled. Most other honorably discharged veterans receive a five-point bonus. A disabled Vietnam veteran receives fifteen points. On any exam, a grade of 70 must be achieved before the preference points are added. The policy of veterans' preference dates back to the Civil War and predates the first Civil Service Act (1883).

Appointments

When an agency has a position to fill, under the "rule of three," the Office of Personnel Management sends three names. The names are those having the top three total points, including veterans' preference. From among these three an appointment will be made without regard to race, color, religion, politics, or sex. A physical handicap will not prevent a person from being hired if it does not interfere with the required duties.

An investigation will be made of the applicant's character, reliability, and trustworthiness. He or she will be asked to swear to support and defend the Constitution of the United States. His or her fingerprints will be taken and checked against the FBI records. Any intentional false statement, doubt about U.S. loyalty, or criminal conduct may prevent a person from getting the appointment.

RIGHTS OF GOVERNMENT EMPLOYEES

Government employees retain most, but not all, of their rights as citizens. Any abridgement of rights may differ by locality, by agency, or by job. For example, a city may require a municipal employee to live within the city limits. Teachers may or may not have the right of collective bargaining and unionization. An employee may be required to have a valid driver's license.

Citizenship is generally required for federal employment, but not necessarily for state and local government employment. There are exceptions, and citizenship may be required for certain positions.

Politics

According to the U.S. Office of Special Counsel, the Hatch Act restricts the political activity of employees of the federal government executive branch and District of Columbia government, as well as some state and local employees who work in connection with federally funded programs. Under the Hatch Act, federal employees may not use their official authority to interfere with an election, solicit or receive political contributions, be candidates for public office in partisan elections, or engage in political activity while on duty or representing the government.

Federal employees may be candidates for office in nonpartisan elections, assist in voter registration drives, and contribute money to political campaigns, among other politically related activities. Employees who violate the Hatch Act can be removed from their positions.

Freedom of Speech

In reviewing the contracts for the C-5A airplane, A. Ernest Fitzgerald, a cost accountant, discovered and disclosed a cost overrun of $2 million. He was fired in 1970 allegedly for economy reasons. He sought review through civil service. It took him six years and a $3.5 million lawsuit to regain employment and recover back pay, court costs, and other expenses.

To what extent does a government employee have the right to criticize government policy? Government interests may restrict complete freedom. Public employees, especially accountants, may have access to highly sensitive information. Various court cases have imposed some restriction on freedom of speech.

Private Life

A government employee may be required to answer questions about his or her private life; however, the questions must be legitimate and relate directly to the job or position. They may pertain to the applicant's associations (organizations) if there are questions about loyalty to the U.S. government. The questions may relate to past criminal activity. A traffic violation would be inconsequential; however, theft or fraud would be a different matter. A government employee's federal income tax returns are subject to audit. No guideline exists to define a governmental employee's conduct off the job.

THE FUTURE

An accountant or auditor working for government can experience challenges as diverse as the goverment itself. Governmental accounting is a major alternative to public accounting for the person who is committed, seeks responsibility, and is self-motivated. The government accountant and auditor can feel that he or she is making a personal contribution in finding ways to improve government operations and the services provided to citizens.

There is a need for qualified accountants in government. A qualified person can have career opportunities. There is a track record of promoting from within. This provides the opportunity to move quickly into challenging positions.

A large number of government employment opportunities for accountants are also projected for the future. This will be increasingly true also at the local level as cities and counties develop more sophisticated accounting and reporting systems.

FEDERAL EMPLOYMENT SERVICE CENTERS

Advice and assistance in all areas of human resources management is available at the following Office of Personnel Management locations, including recruitment, application processing and candidate evaluation, workforce restructuring, downsizing and outplacement assistance, and technical assistance in other areas such as classification and test administration.

Atlanta Services Branch
75 Spring Street SW, Suite 1000
Atlanta, GA 30303
E-mail: Atlanta@opm.gov

Chicago Services Branch
230 S. Dearborn Street, DPN 30-3
Chicago, IL 60604
E-mail: Chicago@opm.gov

Denver Services Branch
12345 Alamada Parkway
P.O. Box 25167
Denver, CO 80225
E-mail: Denver@opm.gov

Kansas City Services Branch
601 E. Twelfth Street, Room 131
Kansas City, MO 64106
E-mail: KansasCity@opm.gov

Norfolk Services Branch
200 Granby Street, Room 500
Norfolk, VA 23510
E-mail: Norfolk@opm.gov

Philadelphia Services Branch
600 Arch Street, Room 3400
Philadelphia, PA 19106
E-mail: Philadelphia@opm.gov

Raleigh Services Branch
4407 Bland Road, Suite 200
Raleigh, NC 27609
E-mail: Raleigh@opm.gov

San Antonio Services Branch
8610 Broadway, Room 305
San Antonio, TX 78217
E-mail: SanAntonio@opm.gov

San Francisco Services Branch
120 Howard Street, Room 735
San Francisco, CA 94105
E-mail: SanFrancisco@opm.gov

Washington Services Branch
1900 E Street NW, Room 2469
Washington, DC 20415
E-mail: Washington@opm.gov

SUGGESTED READING

Government Auditing Standards (Yellow Book). U.S. Government Accountability Office. Washington, D.C.: General Accounting Office, 2003.

Government Policy and Guidance. U.S. Government Accountability Office.
Washington, D.C.: General Accounting Office, 2003.

4

THE ACCOUNTANT FOR NONPROFIT ORGANIZATIONS

A nonprofit organization is one that provides a variety of services for the benefit of the general public on a nonprofit basis. These services are normally in the areas of health, welfare, and community services and are provided for no fee or a small user charge to offset the cost incurred. The services are considered beneficial to the public welfare and, therefore, are supported by public contributions and government funds. Nonprofit organizations are given tax-exempt status. Examples of nonprofit organizations include United Way agencies, many hospitals, universities and colleges, and religious organizations.

The revenue and expenditures of a nonprofit organization may easily involve millions of dollars. Accountants are needed to maintain appropriate records and prepare financial statements for the organization's contributors, directors, and executives, and for the government agencies that regulate them. Most nonprofit organizations have special accounting standards tailored to meet their objectives, the nature of their resources and programs, and their methods of operation. Their financial statements are designed to identify the principal programs and their related costs.

The nonprofit organizations discussed in this chapter are:

- Public school systems
- Colleges and universities
- Hospitals and health-care facilities
- Voluntary health and welfare organizations

These are only a selection from the many nonprofit organizations that employ accountants.

PUBLIC SCHOOL SYSTEMS

A public school system is a group of interrelated elements administered by agencies of a county or city government. This is the broad definition. A public school district is an independent government unit. A district is narrower than a school system. However, these terms are often used interchangeably.

Public schools expend money for a variety of programs other than regular instruction, such as classes designed specifically for the mentally handicapped, for the gifted and talented, for those interested in a vocation, for adults with special interests, and for professional people wishing to continue their education. Expenditures are classified by function: instruction, guidance services, health services, general administration, plant maintenance, and student transportation.

Revenue for these services comes from taxpayers through income and property taxes. Both the taxpayers and the government units disbursing this revenue to the school districts are interested in how the funds are spent and expect accountability for it in the form of accurate financial statements.

Private and independent school systems, like public school systems, have operating budgets involving revenue and disbursements in the millions of dollars.

Financial Director

School systems normally have a financial director who may be called the director of business affairs. In a large school system the positions of financial director and treasurer are separated, while in a small school system the two positions are often combined.

Education. Until recently, the financial director held bachelor's and master's degrees in education and often progressed from teacher to principal to financial director for the school system. In recent years, it has become more common to hire financial directors with backgrounds in business administration and/or accounting.

The financial director has both administrative responsibilities and financial responsibilities.

Administrative responsibilities. The administrative responsibilities may include managing the general operation of the school system under the direction of the superintendent of schools. The financial director must supply the public with information when it is requested. He or she must meet with the teaching and custodial staffs and with the unions. He or she is responsible for supervising the buildings and grounds and for complying with local, state, and federal laws and regulations.

Financial responsibilities. Financial responsibilities include preparation of budgets, financing of capital projects, and meeting interest and principal payments on long-term debt. The financial director continuously monitors the flow of cash. A school system often needs to borrow against tax monies, which are received only twice a year. Excess cash is invested in short-term securities until needed.

The financial director is normally responsible for the accounting of the school system's revenue and expenditures. Federal and state grants must be accounted for in separate funds and not intermingled with general tax revenue. The financial records of special activities, such as food service, bookstores, athletic programs, and transportation, must be kept separate from the general operations. And tax forms must be filed even though the school system has a tax-exempt status.

The position requires someone with an accounting background and expertise and knowledge in specialized areas. The responsibilities of the financial director have become increasingly oriented toward finance and accounting.

Salaries. Salaries for accountants involved in financial planning vary depending on the size and location of the school system. In general, salaries range upward from about $60,000.

The position is full time with the usual fringe benefits of holidays, two to four weeks' vacation, medical and life insurance, and a state pension upon retirement.

As administrator of the school's resources, the financial director reports to the superintendent of schools. The director must provide school officials with information as requested and full and accurate financial reporting.

Treasurer

Originally, the school board treasurer was referred to as clerk of the board of education, a position that required only bookkeeping and clerical skills.

The requirements for the treasurer's position have changed, however. Most state boards of education have imposed new standards, elevating the treasurer's position to an attractive career choice of which few accounting students may be aware. Each state has its own standards as established by its own board of education.

Even in smaller communities the school system is a large employer and therefore has a sizable budget. The budget appropriations for a small rural school district can run well over $1.5 million, compared with $100 million for a metropolitan school district. Much larger school districts, such as those of New York City, Chicago, and Los Angeles, may have billion-dollar budgets. The large dollar inflows and outflows of school districts require qualified accountants to budget and manage the funds. State boards of education also have an interest in more accurate and sophisticated reporting, because much of a school system's revenue is provided by the state.

Educational and experience standards. Many state boards of education are adopting minimum educational and experience standards for their school board treasurers. To be employed as a treasurer, a person probably will have to meet one of several qualifications:

- A bachelor's degree in accounting with training in government accounting, financial report preparation, budgeting, and laws relating to school district budgeting and financing
- An associate degree in accounting with related training
- A bachelor's degree in a field other than accounting, provided at least six quarter hours are completed in accounting, three quarter hours in data processing, and eighteen quarter hours in government accounting and other financial and legal areas
- A high school diploma with three years' experience as a school treasurer or fiscal officer in a government entity. The candidate must have completed six quarter hours in accounting and three quarter hours in data processing, along with other business and finance courses.

As school board treasurers retire and resign, new openings appear. These openings will be filled by qualified accountants.

Responsibilities. The responsibilities of a school board treasurer are equivalent to those of a chief fiscal officer in industry. Varied and challenging duties often include:

- Depositing all monies of the district
- Keeping a record of cash receipts
- Reporting current cash balances to the board of education
- Preparing and distributing invoices
- Signing purchase orders and contracts
- Signing checks to disburse money
- Keeping a record of all expenditures
- Maintaining the payroll function and payroll records
- Preparing and supervising the bidding process for repairs and capital improvements
- Assisting in developing school bond issues and operating levies
- Investing excess funds on a short- and long-term basis
- Assisting the superintendent or financial director in developing the annual budget
- Preparing the resolution for annual legal authorization to spend funds, subject to board approval
- Submitting monthly and annual financial statements to the board
- Submitting the required financial reports to the county auditor, state auditor, and state department of education
- Supervising all personnel in the treasurer's office

Salaries. Salaries of school district treasurers nationwide can have a wide range depending upon the size of the school system. According to the Educational Research Service, administrators for finance and business earned an average of $83,678 during the 2004–2005 year.[1]

A school board treasurer can advance from a small system to a larger school system. Also, an accountant with supervisory experience may transfer from industry to the position of treasurer. The position of school board treasurer is emerging as a new and challenging position for accountants.

COLLEGES AND UNIVERSITIES

By industry standards, many colleges and universities rank as "big business" because of the number of personnel employed, revenue received, and total economic impact upon the community. Such schools employ high-level financial officers to manage accounts.

Treasurer, Controller, and Bursar

Colleges and universities with a sizable enrollment usually have a treasurer, a controller, and a bursar. The treasurer, as chief financial officer, supervises the financial affairs of the institution. The responsibilities are numerous and complex and of a planning and decision-making nature. The treasurer will delegate the function of handling receipts and disbursements of monies to the bursar and the function of recording these receipts and disbursements to the controller. The controller is the chief internal accountant. Figure 4.1 shows the organizational structure and responsibility relationships of the accounting and financial positions within a university. Smaller institutions may combine the three positions into one using one of the three titles, or they may have two positions: treasurer or bursar and controller.

Responsibilities. The responsibilities and duties of a college or university treasurer, controller, and bursar are similar to those of the controller in

Figure 4.1

Accounting Positions with a University or College

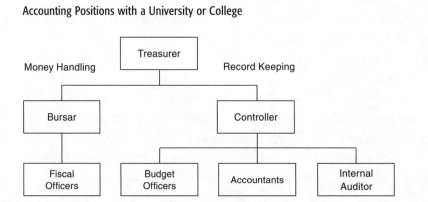

industry and those of the school board treasurer. They are responsible for the financial health of the academic institution.

Some of the treasurer's major duties include:

- Determining and advising the board of trustees regarding short- and long-term financing needs
- Preparing reports for the board of trustees
- Delegating authority for receiving and disbursing funds
- Forecasting the future financial position
- Investment of excess funds

Primary duties of the controller are:

- Responsibility for the accounting function of the university: residence halls, athletics, bookstores, libraries, cafeterias, general instruction, and so forth
- Separate accountability for all funds which are restricted: endowments for scholarships, donations and bequests, and student loans
- Establishment of the annual budget and its incorporation into the accounting system
- Preparing the financial statements of the institution

Educational requirements. A controller and/or treasurer normally holds a bachelor's degree in accounting, is a certified public accountant or a certified management accountant, and has prior experience in public accounting or with another academic institution.

Most colleges and universities require an audit of their annual financial statements. It is natural for an individual who has served as auditor of the institution's records to step from the ranks of public accountant to controller.

Salary. The larger the institution, the higher the salaries may be. The salaries of controllers, treasurers, and bursars in state colleges and universities are affected by state funds available for higher education. They also tend to be comparable with salaries of controllers and treasurers in industry.

The treasurer, controller, and bursar will enjoy the same fringe benefits as the faculty and staff. Medical, dental, and life insurance coverage is provided plus a pension under the state requirement system. A forty-hour workweek is normal and a two- to four-week vacation is provided.

Budget Officer, Fiscal Officer, Accountant

Universities also employ budget officers and fiscal officers, as well as accountants.

Responsibilities. The budget officer is responsible for formulating an annual budget, which may be required by law. Budgets are essential for good management and often are recorded in the accounting systems as legal limitations on expenditures.

A fiscal officer is charged with collecting, managing, and disbursing the institution's funds or revenue.

Accountants perform the routine accounting duties. Their positions are comparable to those of the junior and senior general accountant with industry.

An internal auditor performs a continuous review of the accounting system and assesses the reliability of the financial records. Recommendations are made for improvements to the system.

Salaries. Annual salaries range from the mid- to upper $20,000s for an inexperienced staff accountant in a small institution to over $70,000 for an experienced executive in a large institution.

These positions generally have a forty-hour workweek. Fringe benefits include holidays, vacations, insurance coverage, and a retirement pension similar to those granted other staff members.

HOSPITALS AND HEALTH-CARE FACILITIES

Hospital and health-care facilities are also businesses that must be run efficiently and with an eye to the bottom line. These institutions employ accountants to handle their fiscal matters.

Hospitals

Dramatic changes have taken place in hospital accounting over the last decade. Hospitals have increased the volume and range of their services.

Hospital costs have increased at the same time that support by local governments and philanthropists has decreased. Hospital boards are becoming cost conscious and want to know the costs involved in providing various medical services.

Hospitals may be government units, such as veterans' hospitals; many are affiliated with churches and universities; some are operated by other nonprofit organizations. The American Hospital Association, the Healthcare Financial Management Association, and the AICPA have developed and improved financial accounting and reporting procedures. Audited financial statements are now necessary to support requests for borrowing and for reporting to the state and to other agencies. Certified public accountants are currently exerting greater influence on the reporting practices of hospitals.

The growth of health-care services like BlueCross and Medicare has been a major influence on hospital accounting, since their payment plans contribute a substantial portion of most hospital revenues. Consequently, these third-party payment plans increase the record keeping and auditing required of hospitals and health-care facilities.

Accountants. Hospitals hire bookkeepers and accountants for the same purposes as private industry and provide job classifications comparable with industry as to responsibilities and salaries. A general accountant with less than one year of experience, performing general and cost accounting functions, earned from $30,750 to $36,750 in 2005, according to Robert Half International. A senior accountant, working in the same areas as the junior accountant mentioned above, earned from $44,250 to $55,750.[2]

Vice president of fiscal affairs. The vice president of fiscal affairs is responsible for the financial and managerial department of a hospital. It is an executive position. The vice president will maintain and supervise an accounting department that accounts for routine activities of the hospital; property, plant, and equipment; bequests and endowments; investments; long-term debt; and restricted funds designated for special use by the hospital governing board.

The vice president should have a bachelor's degree in accounting and a master's degree in accounting or business administration and be a certified public accountant.

Salary depends upon the size of the institution and the revenue available. Salaries are comparable to those for the same position with an industrial corporation of the same size.

Budget director. The budget director is responsible for the entire budgetary process and works directly with the department directors in forecasting revenue and in reviewing each line item of expense. The director compiles all departmental budgets into a master budget and supports it with statistical and cost reports. Each month, the budget director prepares a report comparing the budgeted amounts with the actual costs incurred.

The budget director should have a bachelor's degree in accounting with a specialization in hospital and management accounting. The director might be either a certified public accountant or a certified management accountant.

The annual salary for budget director may start at approximately $70,000 a year, depending upon the size of the company or hospital.[3]

Health-care provider auditor. The health-care industry has given rise to a position called provider auditor. BlueCross BlueShield hires auditors to review the cost data submitted by providers of health-care services; that is, hospitals and nursing homes. These provider auditors do the field audits necessary to render an opinion that cost data submitted by the hospital are in accordance with the regulations established by Medicare and Medicaid.

The provider auditor must have a degree in accounting plus two to three years of audit experience. Salaries generally begin around $40,000.

Job Outlook

The job outlook for accountants in the health-care field appears to be very good for the next decade. Population growth, the aging of the baby boomer generation, and increased longevity are some of the factors that will spur the growth of jobs in hospitals, nursing homes, clinics, and special treatment centers such as rehabilitation facilities.

According to the Healthcare Financial Management Association, in 2003 accountants in health-care facilities earned an average salary of $44,800.[4] Employees generally receive fringe benefits including medical and life insurance, paid vacations and sick leave, and paid holidays.

New job opportunities come from a growing number of managed care organizations. All need strong business managers to support their clinical staffs: outpatient clinics, HMOs, and the growing number of health networks. Table 4.1 shows average salaries for health-care CFOs.

Year	Average Salary
1980	$38,300
1984	54,700
1986	56,615
1989	62,600
1991	82,100
1993	85,000
1995	112,800
1999	110,000
2001	127,000
2003	151,000

Source: Healthcare Financial Management Association

Note: HFMA cautions that survey samples and methods differed through the years, and results aren't strictly comparable.

VOLUNTARY HEALTH AND WELFARE ORGANIZATIONS

Voluntary health and welfare organizations (VHWOs) are nonprofit organizations that receive their support primarily from public contributions. They provide various kinds of health, welfare, and community services. Organized for the public benefit, these organizations have a tax-exempt status.

A local VHWO may be affiliated with a national organization that shares the same objectives. The United Way is the most widely known VWHO in the United States, comprising around fourteen hundred community-based organizations. Some of the agencies that are included under the United Way are:

- American Cancer Society
- American Heart Association
- American Red Cross
- Arthritis Foundation
- Boy Scouts of America
- Cystic Fibrosis Foundation
- Girl Scouts of America

- National Kidney Foundation
- Salvation Army
- Young Men's Christian Association (YMCA)
- Young Women's Christian Association (YWCA)

Most United Way agencies submit budgets in return for an allocation from voluntary contributions given annually by businesses and their employees. For example, the American Cancer Society signs a contract with the United Way for a specified amount and, in return, does not solicit business donations.

These agencies have extensive accounting systems designed by the United Way of America. Their income is derived from public support in the form of contributions and special events, fees and grants from government agencies, and other sources. Their accounting systems must differentiate between sources of revenue. They must also account for land, building and equipment, endowment funds for gifts and bequests, and endowment fund investments. This revenue is designated for the various programs and functions of the agency. Budgets are incorporated into these agency accounting systems because of concern with the use of future resources. Agency financial statements are provided for contributors, the organization's trustees or directors, the executives of the VHWO, and for the governments that regulate it.

Fiscal Officer

Each of these agencies has an officer responsible for its fiscal operations. That person usually carries the title of fiscal officer, although sometimes it is accounting manager, controller, or financial administrator.

Qualifications. The fiscal officer usually holds a graduate degree, either a master's in business administration or a master's in public administration that is accounting oriented or combined with a bachelor's degree in accounting. The fiscal officer often has had employment experience with a corporation and/or a health-care facility. The individual must be bondable and often is a certified public accountant.

Responsibilities. The accounting responsibilities of the financial (fiscal) officer are:

- To maintain daily control of receivables and cash
- To prepare monthly financial statements for the board of trustees, the United Way, and outside auditor, and/or any other interested parties
- To prepare operating budgets and to compare them monthly with expenditures
- To use a cost system to determine hourly costs of programs provided
- To maintain internal control and meet all auditing requirements
- To comply with policies established by the board of trustees and with all legal requirements that may affect the agency's operation

The fiscal (financial) officer is both an accountant and a manager and, as such, has both types of duties to perform. Additional duties that are administrative, rather than accounting in nature, include:

- Supervising all fiscal staff members
- Conducting finance and investment committee meetings
- Attending board meetings and all other committee meetings
- Reviewing and updating manuals as needed
- Reviewing personnel data and reporting results of the salary survey to committee

Salary and benefits. Salaries range from $35,000 on up depending upon experience, whether the fiscal officer is a certified public accountant, and length of service. All benefits are fully paid, including insurance, hospitalization, and retirement benefits. The agencies are liberal in granting vacations and provide the usual paid holidays.

Only in recent years have VHWOs begun hiring accountants to handle their financial needs and systems. The United Way and the AICPA have upgraded and prescribed specialized accounting systems for VHWOs. As accounting literature has become specialized in the nonprofit sector, many new positions have become available for accountants. Nonprofit organizations need and hire accountants to maintain accurate accounting records, to prepare financial statements, and to file tax reports. As a result, the growth of the nonprofit sector nationwide has created many positions for accountants.

Other Nonprofit Organizations

Other types of nonprofit organizations are:

- Cemetery organizations
- Civic organizations
- Country clubs
- Fraternal organizations
- Labor unions
- Libraries
- Museums
- Performing arts organizations
- Political parties
- Religious organizations

These organizations may or may not be large enough to employ a full-time accountant. When they do hire accountants, the duties and responsibilities are similar to those discussed for voluntary health and welfare organizations.

NOTES

1. ers.org/CATALOG/salarysnapshot2004-2005.pdf (accessed July 5, 2005).
2. *2005 Salary Guide*, Robert Half International, Inc., 10.
3. *Healthcare Financial Management*, July 2003, findarticles.com/p/articles/mi_m3257/is_7_57/ai_105501153 (accessed July 6, 2005).
4. Ibid.

SUGGESTED READING

Gross, Malvern J., Richard F. Larkin, and John H. McCarthy. *Financial and Accounting Guide for Not-for-Profit Organizations.* 6th Ed. New York: Wiley, 2000.

Larkin, Richard F. and Marie DiTommaso. *Wiley Not-for-Profit GAAP 2005: Interpretation and Application of Generally Accepted Accounting Principles for Not-for-Profit Organizations.* New York: Wiley, 2004.

Ruppel, Warren. *Not-for-Profit Accounting Made Easy.* New York: Wiley, 2002.

C H A P T E R

5

THE SOLE PRACTITIONER

The accountant who works as a sole practitioner is owner of the business and operates with no professional staff. Office personnel could include a secretary and bookkeepers. Often the practice is a closely held family business.

Sole practitioners, as a whole, are not a homogeneous group. Their clients vary from small- to medium-sized businesses and from service to retailing companies. Their areas of specialization vary from concentrating on certain related businesses to handling a wide variety of clients. Sole practitioners also vary as to the type of practice. Some engage primarily in write-up work (bookkeeping) using computerized systems, others have primarily a tax practice, and still others may provide a mix of services.

Some sole practitioners are certified public accountants (CPAs) and some are public accountants (PAs). The sole practitioner's chances for having a successful practice are greater if he or she is a certified public accountant.

QUALIFICATIONS

The successful sole practitioner needs certain personal qualifications, technical skills, management skills, and marketing skills.

High on the list of personal qualifications is integrity. The accountant, both CPA and PA, must abide by a code of professional ethics. Information divulged by the client is confidential, and the accountant must treat it as such. Patience is needed to deal with the many problems that can arise. A nice personality coupled with a certain amount of aggressiveness is needed in serving the client's needs. The sole practitioner should enjoy working with people and have the self-confidence necessary to handle the wide variety of tasks encountered.

Sole practitioners are like family physicians. They are individualists who function alone because they choose to do so. They provide high-quality personal services to their clients. They tailor their practices to suit their personalities, family responsibilities, health, and lifestyles.

Technical skills include being knowledgeable in accounting practices and procedures, taxation, management consulting activities, and computers. The accountant should be mathematically inclined and possess the ability to think logically in solving clients' problems. Equally important are oral and written communication skills. In working with clients, members of the community, and others, the accountant needs highly developed communication skills.

From a management viewpoint, the accountant must be able to handle responsibility. The sole practitioner must use his or her own judgment in making decisions and must be willing to accept the responsibility for these decisions. Unless the sole practitioner has a one-person office, he or she will have employees to supervise. It requires organization and planning to develop and use the talents of the employees most efficiently. The sole practitioner must be a manager.

Last, but not least, marketing skills are necessary to help the practice grow. Marketing skills include the ability to sell oneself and one's talents, and some involvement in community activities. Participation in community activities is necessary to establish contact with bankers, attorneys, and other professional people who work within the community.

TYPES OF SERVICES RENDERED

The sole practitioner, limited by the lack of accounting personnel within his or her own firm, can render services only for small- and medium-sized business entities. The services rendered will fall into one or more of the following areas:

- Accounting and write-up work
- Compilation and review
- Tax services

- Management advisory services
- Audit services

Accounting and Write-Up Work

Most small firms do some accounting and write-up work. Write-up work includes recording transactions in books of original entry (called *journals*), transferring amounts from the journals to a ledger (called *posting*), reconciliation of bank statements, monthly adjustments, financial statement preparation, and filing of sales and payroll tax reports. This write-up work, commonly called bookkeeping, does not command the higher fees that other types of service generate. Too much write-up work will require the sole practitioner to put in longer and longer hours to make a satisfactory income, not leaving time for the practitioner to build his or her professional competence. Today much of this work is computerized and, thus, the sole practitioner can train someone in his or her own or the client's office to do this work. Write-up work should be considered a stepping-stone to services requiring skills, such as tax work and consulting.

Write-up work often leads to the preparation of unaudited financial statements for clients. In past years considerable confusion existed as to what procedures should be used in issuing unaudited financial statements. How much work should the accountant undertake? What is his or her responsibility for these statements that he or she prepared? A number of lawsuits were brought against independent accountants. To answer these questions, the AICPA appointed an accounting and review services committee to study the problem and issue recommendations on nonaudit services rendered to business entities. This committee recommended that unaudited financial statements be replaced with compilations and reviews of financial statements.

Compilation and Review

A report must be issued upon completion of a compilation or review and when financial statements are issued. Unlike an audit, a compilation report expresses no assurance about the financial statements, and a review report expresses limited assurance.

A compilation requires no audit procedures. Instead, the accountant performs accounting services for the client, such as adjusting the books and preparing the financial statements. As a minimum, the accountant must have a general understanding of the nature of the client's business transactions, the accounting records, and the format of the financial statements. He or she must also develop sufficient knowledge about the entity's industry in order to compile financial statements that are consistent with industry practice. The accountant's report should accompany the compiled financial statements (which should conform to generally accepted accounting principles). This report describes the scope of the work performed by the accountant, including any limitations. The report stipulates that the financial statements are the representation of management, that they have not been audited or reviewed, and that no opinion or other form of assurance is given on them.

A review contains a limited assurance that the financial statements contain no material departures from generally accepted accounting principles. To give a limited assurance on the financial statements, the accountant must make inquiries and perform analytical procedures. Examples of some of the inquiries and procedures performed are:

- Ensure that the entity has applied generally accepted accounting principles.
- Review the procedures for recoding the transactions.
- Compare the financial statement with those of prior periods.
- Review actions taken by the board of directors and the stockholders.
- Review the financial statements for conformity to generally accepted accounting principles.

After reviewing the financial statements, the accountant prepares a report that a review was performed in accordance with AICPA standards and that the financial statements are the representation of management (owners). The nature of the review is described. The report should state that a review is substantially less than an audit. And finally, a negative assurance is given; that is, the accountant is not aware of any material departures from generally accepted accounting principles. If there are any such departures, they must be disclosed in the accountant's report.

Tax Services

Tax work generally accounts for a high percentage of the work performed by sole practitioners. Tax services include preparing and filing federal, state, and local tax returns for individuals and small business clients. Tax services also include tax planning, advising clients of legitimate means of reducing taxes, and estate planning.

Certified public accountants may represent their clients before the Internal Revenue Service. A public accountant may qualify by taking a special enrollment examination given annually each fall in an IRS district. An application with fee must be filed with the IRS prior to taking the two-day exam.

The sole practitioner who places heavy emphasis on providing tax services will work long hours during the tax season, which extends from January 1 through April 15 each year. Extensions on some tax returns will lengthen the tax season. Tax work, with its many complexities, commands a higher fee than write-up work.

Management Advisory Services

Management advisory services are services of a general business or financial nature not falling under one of the special categories. Some examples are designing and implementing a cost system, selecting and installing a computer system, improving the accounting system, assistance on hiring and training accounting personnel, assistance in obtaining a bank loan, and special analyses to aid the client in achieving certain objectives.

Audit Services

At most, audit services form a small percentage of the sole practitioner's business. The practitioner will be able to undertake only small audit engagements that can be completed within a limited time frame. An example is the small business whose banker requests an audit prior to granting a loan.

An audit is a review of the accounting records of a business entity and the issuance of an audit report stating that the financial reports issued by the entity fairly present its financial position and are prepared in accordance with generally accepted accounting principles. For a fuller discussion of auditing, refer to Chapter 1.

STARTING AND BUILDING A PRACTICE

The accountant starting his or her own practice risks an uncertain future. Sacrifices in time, in effort, and in finances are made. Financial rewards will build slowly because initially the sole practitioner will get those clients wanting time-consuming, low-paying bookkeeping services. The accountant building a practice will need time and effort to manage his or her own firm. The accountant enjoying newfound independence and the challenge of building a practice will require self-reliance, self-discipline, and the ability to withstand discouragement.

Factors to Consider

Before starting a practice, you should talk with other sole practitioners. The single most common cause of failure is lack of sufficient experience. You should be employed first by another firm and gain several years' experience before opening your own practice. The sole practitioner should have been employed by a corporation, a public accounting firm, or the government at a supervisory level.

Keeping in mind his or her training and experience, the accountant should consider the following factors:

- The type of practice that can be built (tax, bookkeeping, financial planning, specialized clientele, or a varied practice)
- The amount of revenue needed to replace earnings lost through leaving employment elsewhere
- The means of attracting and gaining new clients
- The amount of financing needed in the early years and how much borrowing will be necessary
- Where and when the practice should be opened
- The available market for accounting services

Revenue

It can be very difficult for the accountant to forecast revenue for the first year. Theoretically a budget should be prepared based on the estimated number of billable hours multiplied by established hourly rates for the different services to be rendered. Unless the accountant has a major client or several good clients when starting out, however, billable hours is really an unknown. In practice, many factors will operate to prevent normal billing. Some of these factors are unbillable review and research time, lack of experience, low-level clientele billed at the lowest rates, clients who do not or cannot pay, clients who dispute billings to obtain low fees, and hours written off on first-time clients. Accountants with more experience can charge higher rates.

Business expenditures will be made for furniture, fixtures and equipment, and for operating expenses. Operating expenses include rent, insurance, a tax library, utilities, telephone, supplies, the salary of support personnel, professional dues and license, and continuing education seminars. Computers, furniture, fixtures, and equipment can cost from $2,000 up. Operating expenses can be significantly less if you work out of your home, or they can range from $4,000 to $7,500 a month if you start your own business and work from an outside office. Establishing an office in one's home does not give a professional image, but it may be an economic necessity for a year or two.

Revenue minus the costs of buying furniture and equipment and minus operating expenses leaves very little for living expenses. The accountant may need to borrow during the early years of starting a practice.

Some options include renting equipment rather than buying, sharing office space with another professional, and earning supplemental income by teaching a night class in accounting at a nearby university. The rule of thumb is that it takes five years to become self-supporting. Some accountants have accomplished it in three years.

Sources of Clients

Networking is vital to an individual opening a new practice. Friends, family, professional colleagues, and other contacts can be a valuable source of new business. An announcement containing a business card should be sent to current clients, lawyers, bankers, business acquaintances, friends, organizations, former associates, insurance agencies, and real estate agents. Most clients are obtained through referral from someone else. Criteria considered important in building and maintaining clientele include personal service (attention), reputation, experience, and the range of services offered.

Some involvement in community activity is desirable. The sole practitioner should also be active in a professional organization at the local level to maintain contact with other accountants.

The sole practitioner should have good communication with his or her clients. This communication may be strengthened by sending newsletters and tax tips, and by telephone calls. An open line of communication often leads to additional services. It may prevent the loss of a client because of recession, bankruptcy, and other causes. Clients are lost because they outgrow the services offered by the accountant, they are bought out by a larger company, or they require services the accountant cannot perform due to lack of staff.

Location and Time

The office preferably should be in an area where other businesses are located. Location is an influential factor in a client's choice of an accounting firm. Location in a good business district provides contact with potential clients. An alternative, should such a location be too costly, is to share space with another CPA, an attorney, an insurance agent, or another professional person. Larger communities provide greater opportunities for the growth of a practice than small communities.

Early fall, September and October, is the best time to open a new office. The accountant has time to furnish and establish an office, send out announcements, make contacts, and get ready for the tax season. Many new clients are obtained during tax season, January 1 to April 15, when tax returns must be filed.

Advantages

The sole practitioner has the advantage of determining the quality of his or her work life. An unhurried lifestyle, freedom to be one's own boss, personal involvement in all areas of accounting, the challenge of managing a practice, and more time to enjoy life are the most common rewards cited for operating as a sole practitioner. A practice can be designed to fit one's health limitations without inconveniencing anyone. An individual practice can provide flexible hours for the person entering accounting who wishes to have time for family.

The sole proprietor has a personal involvement that is becoming increasingly rare in the accounting field. He or she becomes a trusted friend and consultant to many of the small-business-owner clients in the community. This role goes far beyond balancing the books and preparing financial statements. In a small town the accountant's role can be very broad. Examples of consulting services performed for clients may include advice in:

- Buying or selling a business
- Providing for succession of ownership
- Pricing of products or services for sale
- Financial statement analysis resulting in improved profitability

The practitioner's income level may be lower than that of the accountant in industry or in public accounting. He or she may drive a smaller car, own a smaller home, and take less exotic vacations. On the other hand, the practitioner with high-level clients in sound financial condition can enjoy the rewards of economic success: car, home, and social status.

Disadvantages and Dangers

There are many disadvantages of having one's own practice, and the most common fall into three basic categories:

- Limited business growth
- Lack of shared responsibility
- Lack of a balanced lifestyle

The growth of the practice is limited by the owner's knowledge, billable hours, and energy level. The owner takes on all decision making and the management of the practice. The owner must take time to keep abreast of tax law changes, keep up with a growing number of technical and professional rules and guidelines, gain expertise in new areas, learn new methods, and acquire new equipment. Reading and monitoring the new rules, plus running the office, can take up more than 50 percent of the sole practitioner's time. All this reduces time spent on billable accounting services for clients. Only so much can be delegated to an assistant. The sole practitioner also loses billable time when attending seminars and conventions. The total cost for such days equals the cost of the seminar plus the loss of billable services.

The job can be physically and emotionally draining from January through April. The practitioner often works one hundred–hour weeks. Clients call at all hours of the day and night with business and family crises.

Sole practitioners will face difficulties due to compulsory continuing professional education requirements, the costs of peer review, the cost and unavailability of liability insurance, increased marketing costs, and prob-

93
The Sole
Practitioner

lems attracting and retaining qualified staff. A practitioner with a practice that is not state-of-the-art might have difficulty selling the business at retirement.

Sole practitioners often have no one to turn to for advice and discussion of problems that emerge. They have no one to review their work, no one to delegate responsibility to, no one to help take on opportunities. In the event of illness, disability, or death, they must carefully plan for a successor who has the necessary skills to carry on the accounting practice.

It will be difficult for the practitioner to separate business and home life. It will be difficult to take a vacation and leave someone else to manage the office. It will be difficult to be efficient, stay well, and keep some personal time. Handling stress and living a balanced life are necessary to maintain high productivity.

THE FUTURE

In the past, individual practices, like many small businesses, have experienced growth without a lot of planning. This growth rate may be slowing because of a changing economic environment. Since most individual practices are primarily a combination of write-up services and preparation of tax returns, they are vulnerable to the competition offered by large organizations such as banks, service bureaus, and tax service organizations. Rivalry from these nonaccounting sources introduces price competition and a shrinking market.

Small firms are often "wedded" to their small clients. If the accounting firm grows, it will do so more because of its clients' growth than because the firm has acquired a greater number of clients. The quality of service rendered is very important, as is the personal interaction between client and firm.

Small firms must plan for growth. They must take the same advice they give to clients. They must practice management skills, marketing skills, and anticipate the needs of the business environment. Good administration is essential to a successful practice.

The individual practitioner of the future may need to develop a specialization. The specialization might be in computerized systems, divorce cases and complex settlements, cash flow and budgeting, financing methods and opportunities, pension plans, estate planning, insurance adequacy studies, or accounting for professional athletes. Technical specialties will arise within the accounting profession. The accountant of the future will be more of a thinker and less of a doer.

SUGGESTED READING

Carter, Gary W. *Getting Started in Tax Consulting.* New York: Wiley, 2001.

Fox, Jack. *Starting and Building Your Own Accounting Business.* 3rd ed. New York: Wiley, 2000.

Weiss, Alan. *How to Acquire Clients: Powerful Techniques for the Successful Practitioner.* San Francisco: Pfeiffer, 2002.

CHAPTER 6

THE ACCOUNTING EDUCATOR AND ADMINISTRATOR

Teachers impart knowledge, give instruction, and guide by example. Teachers also develop the mental powers of their students. Good teachers, by sharing their knowledge and enthusiasm for a given subject, can profoundly influence the lives of their students. Teachers of accounting are found at three levels: high school, business and community college, and the university.

This chapter will discuss the accounting educator at these three levels and explore environments, qualifications, salaries, employment opportunities, and work satisfaction.

HIGH SCHOOL ACCOUNTING TEACHER

High school accounting teachers work with young people going through the transition from childhood to adulthood. They teach a subject in more depth than it is taught in elementary school. The high school student is undergoing physical and emotional changes and is beginning to consider his or her future employment or career. The high school teacher plays a direct role in this process.

A typical high school curriculum includes two full-year courses called Accounting 1 and 2 or Bookkeeping 1 and 2, which are offered at the junior and senior levels. The teacher develops lesson plans; prepares, gives, and grades tests; arranges for classroom speakers; and organizes other activities. In some schools the teacher designs the classroom assignments to meet the individual needs and abilities of the students. The high school teacher may conduct as many as five separate accounting classes per day.

In addition to teaching assignments, high school teachers supervise study halls and homerooms, schedule meetings with parents and school counselors, and serve as faculty advisers for accounting clubs or Future Business Leaders of America (FBLA). Teachers are expected to attend workshops and college classes to remain current in their specialties and on trends in education.

Some schools hire teacher aides to help with routine tasks and paper grading. While this helps, most teachers still work a minimum of forty hours a week. Sometimes student teachers are available from nearby colleges. These student teachers provide assistance and, in return, receive guidance and classroom experience.

Qualifications

The educational requirement for teaching accounting at the high school level is a four-year bachelor's degree in business education. The business classes needed to obtain this degree vary from state to state. Most states require that the student take at least three accounting courses, in addition to courses in management, marketing, economics, mathematics, and data processing.

Approved colleges and universities in every state offer the courses and the student-teaching experience required by the state. Each of the fifty states and the District of Columbia require that public high school teachers be certified. (Many states also require certification of private and parochial high school teachers.) Information on educational requirements may be obtained from each state's department of education or the nearest accredited university or college that offers a program in business education.

Salary

Salaries of beginning high school teachers vary from state to state and also from school district to school district within a state. Large school systems can usually pay higher salaries than small school systems. School systems that have a high tax base because of the presence of industry or other factors often can offer higher salaries than school systems in entirely residential or agricultural settings. Salaries also tend to be higher in the northeastern and western parts of the United States.

According to the National Association of Colleges and Employers (NACE), in 2004 bachelor's degree candidates with majors in secondary education received an average starting salary of $30,646. Accounting majors averaged $41,058.[1] Higher salaries are based on education and length of service in the educational system. Factors that will increase a teacher's salary are additional certification, a master's degree, and length of service.

In some school systems the accounting teacher has the opportunity to serve as school treasurer and can earn additional compensation from this source. The high school teacher sometimes teaches evening education courses in accounting when the school system offers those classes. This also provides supplemental income.

Employment Opportunities

Job opportunities for teachers in general are expected to vary from good to excellent over the next ten years, depending on location and subject. Most job openings will be attributable to the expected retirement of a large number of teachers. In addition, relatively high rates of turnover, especially among beginning teachers employed in poor, urban schools, also will lead to numerous job openings for teachers. Competition for qualified teachers among some localities will likely continue, with schools luring teachers from other states and districts with bonuses and higher pay.

Increasing enrollments of minorities, coupled with a shortage of minority teachers, should cause efforts to recruit minority teachers to intensify. Also, the number of non-English-speaking students has grown dramatically, creating demand for bilingual teachers. The supply of teachers is expected to increase in response to reports of improved job prospects, better pay, more teacher involvement in school policy, and greater public interest in education.

In recent years, the total number of bachelor's and master's degrees granted in education has increased steadily. Because of a shortage of teachers in certain locations, and in anticipation of the loss of a number of teachers to retirement, many states have implemented policies that will encourage more students to become teachers. In addition, more teachers may be drawn from a reserve pool of career changers, substitute teachers, and teachers completing alternative certification programs.

Work Satisfaction

People who like to work with young people can find high school teaching a very satisfying experience. Men and women who prefer to be employed during the hours their children are in school are likely to find teaching very rewarding. Teaching enables parents to be home with their families during the summer and during the spring and winter breaks. It also provides time for travel and other enriching activities.

BUSINESS AND COMMUNITY COLLEGE TEACHERS

Business and community college faculty teach more mature students than the high school teacher does. Most business and community colleges offer two-year programs and degrees. They provide their students with training for specific vocations.

The accounting program at these institutions does not provide a full range of accounting courses. Most programs offer courses in principles of accounting (the introductory course), financial accounting (reporting to outsiders: stockholders, bankers, creditors), cost accounting (managerial decision making), and accounting for individual income taxes. The student is prepared for a paraprofessional position in the accounting world.

A teacher at the business and community college primarily teaches, gives and grades tests, and counsels students. The business college teacher conducts several classes a day. Community college teachers may teach on a similar basis or may teach several classes that meet only two or three times per week. The difference arises when the community college is part of a university system. The business and community colleges have faculty that specialize in teaching certain courses. Faculty members can expect to work from thirty-five to forty hours per week.

If the community college is part of a university system, the teaching situation and experience will more closely resemble teaching at a university. Many community college faculty engage in research and publish their findings in professional journals.

Qualifications

The minimum requirement to teach in a business or community college is a four-year degree with a major in accounting from an accredited university. However, master's degree holders fill most full-time positions, and CPA certification is recommended for promotion. With increasing competition for available jobs, institutions can be more selective in their hiring practices. Many two-year institutions increasingly prefer job applicants to have some teaching experience or experience with distance learning. Preference also may be given to those holding dual master's degrees, because they can teach more subjects. In addition, with greater competition for jobs, master's degree holders may find it increasingly difficult to obtain employment as they are passed over in favor of candidates holding a Ph.D.

Salary

Private business schools, like high schools, do not assign faculty ranks. Salary increases are determined by education (master's degree or higher), CPA certification, and length of service.

A community college that is not part of a university system may or may not assign rank to its faculty. The ranks, in ascending order, are instructor, assistant professor, associate professor, and professor. These positions are discussed more fully in the university section of this chapter.

Salary and compensation for two-year colleges with ranks are given in Table 6.1. Again, salaries for the same rank will vary by institution, by state (because of differences in state funding), and by geographic region.

Table 6.1 Salaries of College and University Faculty Members, 2002–2003
(Average salary, all disciplines)

Two-Year College Faculty	40th Percentile	20th Percentile
Professor	$57,468	$52,350
Associate professor	48,621	43,990
Assistant professor	40,813	37,955
Instructor	35,284	33,061
University Professors	**40th Percentile**	**20th Percentile**
Professor	$51,065	$57,255
Associate professor	43,470	48,060
Assistant professor	38,225	41,188
Instructor	31,819	35,073

Source: *The Chronicle of Higher Education*, AAUP Faculty Salary Survey 2003.

Employment Opportunities

Since the late 1980s, business and community colleges have reported annual gains in enrollment. Lack of employment and a tight job market led many students to return to school to upgrade their job skills. A business or community college appeals to many because the programs prepare them for specific jobs, because it is closer to their homes, or because the tuition is more reasonable.

To accommodate projected increasing enrollments, business and community colleges in many parts of the country are expanding their facilities and hiring additional teachers. An individual possessing the proper credentials may find employment here.

UNIVERSITY ACCOUNTING FACULTY

The main function of the accounting faculty member at an accredited four-year university is to present an in-depth study of the theory and practice of accounting. The faculty member may teach by lecture, discussion, and other means. Lectures may be held in large classrooms accommodating hundreds of students or in seminars containing only a few students. Teaching aids, such as computers, closed-circuit television, and overhead projectors are frequently used. Faculty must publish their research in scholarly journals.

The accounting faculty member usually specializes in one area of accounting. The primary areas are financial, managerial, tax, auditing, and not-for-profit organizations.

Financial accounting is taught in the introductory accounting course (also known as beginning accounting or principles of accounting), intermediate, and advanced accounting. Financial accounting deals with accounting principles and the understanding of financial statements prepared for stockholders, bankers, creditors, and others outside the business entity.

Managerial accounting encompasses costs, budgeting, decision making, and reports and information generated for internal use by company management.

Tax accounting covers taxation for individuals, partnerships, corporations, estates, trusts, tax planning, and tax research.

Auditing includes accounting systems, electronic data processing, computers, and computer programming.

Not-for-profit accounting covers local, state, and federal governments; hospitals; universities; voluntary health and welfare organizations; and many other nonprofit entities that use a specialized system known as fund accounting.

College faculty generally have fewer hours assigned to classroom teaching because of the emphasis on conducting research and publishing. Research is an important part of the work of the university faculty member. At universities offering doctorates, faculty members are heavily involved in research activities.

Service to the university and community carries less emphasis but is also highly regarded. University service includes committee assignments, curriculum studies and revisions, and counseling students. The faculty member may represent the university in the community by serving on the boards of various organizations, such as United Appeal or Mobile Meals.

Qualifications

A master's in business administration (M.B.A.) or master's in accounting degree combined with a CPA certificate or CMA (Certified Management Accountant) certificate is the minimum requirement for employment in a university offering a four-year program in accounting. A person with these qualifications is hired at the rank of lecturer or instructor, usually for a maximum of three or four years.

A person whose goal is to become a college professor should complete a Ph.D. program or a doctorate in business administration (D.B.A.) in accounting. The doctorate requires a dissertation involving original research in an area of accounting specialization. Doctoral programs usually take four to seven years of full-time study beyond the bachelor's degree. The dissertation, done under the guidance of a faculty adviser, usually takes one or two years of full-time work.

A Ph.D. or D.B.A. with no experience usually will be hired at the assistant professor level in either an undergraduate or graduate school. Graduate schools are those that offer master's or doctoral programs; they require their faculty to hold doctorates. Newly hired faculty serve a certain period, usually five to seven years, under temporary contracts. At the end of the contract period, their record of teaching, research, and service is reviewed. A favorable review results in the granting of tenure.

Over the last two decades, colleges and universities have employed an increasing number of adjunct faculty, professionals without doctoral degrees or teaching experience who teach part-time. Some institutions offer limited-term contracts to prospective faculty. These contracts, generally for two, three, or five years of full-time employment, may be terminated or extended upon expiration. Institutions are not obligated to grant tenure to the contract holders. In addition, some schools have limited the percentage of faculty who can be tenured.

In addition to the educational requirements needed for a university teaching position, the following factors play an important role in the hiring process:

- Impressions made during the personal interview
- Recommendations
- Graduate school record
- Caliber of university attended
- Quality of doctoral thesis
- Publications
- Ability to conduct research
- Professional involvement

A combination of these factors will determine the employment level, undergraduate or graduate, and the starting rank. In ascending order, university positions are instructor, assistant professor, associate professor, and professor.

Salary

The American Association of University Professors conducts an anual study of two-year, four-year and graduate school faculty salaries. The results of the study, showing average salaries for all disciplines for 2003–2004, are shown in Table 6.2. The data is taken from 1,446 institutions and reflects all affiliations (public, private-independent, and church-related). Average salaries are higher in some areas of the country.

In addition to salary, supplementary income for the university teacher is available from:

- Teaching summer school
- Teaching seminars and adult continuing education courses
- Textbook royalties
- Teaching CPA and CMA review courses
- Consulting for industry
- Research through grant monies

Table 6.2 Salaries of College and University Faculty Members, 2003–2004
(average salary, all disciplines and affiliations)

TWO-YEAR COLLEGE FACULTY

Professor	$64,242
Associate professor	51,720
Assistant professor	45,027
Lecturer	43,290
Instructor	38,747
No rank	36,384
All combined	50,832

UNIVERSITY FACULTY (DOCTORATE HOLDERS)

Professor	$100,682
Associate professor	68,640
Assistant professor	58,576
Lecturer	45,763
Instructor	39,476
No rank	50,711
All combined	75,863

UNIVERSITY FACULTY (MASTER'S HOLDERS)

Professor	$76,112
Associate professor	60,011
Assistant professor	49,959
Lecturer	42,993
Instructor	37,700
No rank	45,625
All combined	59,400

Source: American Association of University Professors,
aaup.org/surveys/04z/surveytab4.pdf, accessed June 13, 2005.

Evaluation, Tenure, and Promotion

A person teaching at the college level is typically evaluated at least once a year. This evaluation becomes the basis for the annual salary increase, for tenure, and for promotion to a higher rank. Tenure is that point at which a professor is granted job security. After tenure is granted, a faculty member cannot be removed without just cause. Different institutions grant tenure at different years of service for different ranks.

The basic criteria used in this evaluation process are teaching, publishing, professional activities, and service to the university and the community. Each area is weighted, with the highest percentages usually allocated to teaching and publishing—those criteria valued most highly. The weightings will vary at different institutions.

Evaluation in the area of teaching includes the ability to communicate knowledge to students, to stimulate their thinking, to motivate their performance, and to increase their desire to learn. These areas are difficult to evaluate in a concrete, quantitative manner. Other considerations in the evaluation are the level and number of courses taught, development of new courses, and innovative teaching methods.

Professors are expected to devote a certain amount of time to research and, as a result of their research, to publish articles and books in their related fields. Editorships and staff positions on professional journals are desirable.

Presenting papers, giving speeches, and attending seminars all contribute to a professor's professional activities. Valuable experience and contacts are gained by accepting an office or chairing a committee for a professional organization.

The American Accounting Association (AAA) is an organization existing specifically for educators. The AAA encourages accounting research. It holds regional and national meetings each year. Other recognized professional organizations include:

- The state societies for certified public accountants
- The American Woman's Society of CPAs (AWSCPA)
- The National Association of Accountants (NAA)
- The American Society of Women Accountants (ASWA)
- The Financial Executives Institute (FEI)

Most of these organizations have local chapters or groups that may be contacted through their national headquarters as listed in Appendix A.

Examples of service to the university include chairing and serving on committees within the department, college, or university. Serving as an officer or faculty advisor to an organization such as Beta Alpha Psi, the accounting honorary, is desirable.

Faculty members are encouraged to be active in the community. They may speak before civic groups, belong to and participate in community organizations, and serve as directors on boards of community agencies.

All these criteria are considered in granting tenure, promotion, and merit salary increases. One additional factor may enter the promotion process. Some universities or colleges require a minimum time in a given rank before one can be promoted to a higher rank.

Employment Opportunities

University teaching positions in accounting are available, and qualified applicants are in demand nationwide. The American Accounting Association website listed over two hundred positions available in colleges throughout the United States and Canada for the 2005–2006 academic year. The areas in greatest demand were financial accounting, managerial accounting, auditing, and general accounting education.

Work Satisfaction

The university professor enjoys a stimulating and challenging environment. Most educators find that the environment encourages professional growth, and their satisfaction comes from independence, self-expression, service to others, stability of employment, opportunity for advancement, good salaries, and availability of positions. Serving as a role model and providing career guidance to students are also sources of personal satisfaction.

Flexible time schedules enable faculty members to engage in a variety of activities. It provides time for research and consulting within the community. Relevant outside experience is considered valuable knowledge that enhances classroom teaching.

At many universities a faculty member has the option of teaching summer classes at additional compensation. Otherwise, the summer months are free for travel, for research and writing, or for additional study. A sabbatical may be requested to pursue a research project. This frees the faculty member from teaching duties, although at a reduced salary. Faculty members are entitled to regular sabbaticals. Most institutions require a minimum number of years of teaching before a faculty member can apply for a sabbatical.

Certain fringe benefits are unique. A faculty member can take additional undergraduate course work free of charge at most universities. Some institutions permit an educator's spouse and children to obtain a bachelor's degree tuition-free.

The usual benefits of medical and dental insurance, life insurance, and retirement plans are provided.

THE ACADEMIC ADMINISTRATOR

In this text, academic administrator refers to the chairperson of the accounting department at a community college or university, or the administrator of a business college.

The academic administrator has a difficult and complex task. The teaching functions may be reduced or eliminated to provide time for handling the many responsibilities that go with administering a department or college. These responsibilities include attending numerous meetings, staying abreast of curriculum changes, hiring new faculty, negotiating the budget, and handling public relations.

At some colleges and universities, the department chairperson holds a five-year position that is rotated among faculty members. Some faculty welcome the position as a change from grading papers and the routine of classroom preparation. However, scholarly pursuits are often relinquished during these periods.

The role of administrator requires management skills, which should be developed early. These skills include developing budgets, writing statements of objectives, learning methods of evaluation, and delegating tasks. An educator aspiring to the administrative ranks must demonstrate the skills required of a top executive.

NOTES

1. *Nace Salary Survey* 43, no. 4 (Fall 2004): 4.

SUGGESTED READING

Albrecht, W. Steve. *Accounting Education: Charting the Course Through a Perilous Future.* Sarasota, FL: American Accounting Association, 2000.

Schwartz, Bill N., and J. Edward Ketz. *Advances in Accounting Education Teaching and Curriculum Innovations.* Greenwich, CT: JAI Press, 2005.

CHAPTER 7

THE FINANCIAL PLANNER

Interested in adding a specialty to your practice? Financial analysis and personal financial planning are growing fields that many accountants and CPAs are choosing as areas of specialization.

These specialists provide analysis and guidance to businesses and individuals to help them with their investment decisions. Both types of specialist gather financial information, analyze it, and make recommendations to their clients. However, their job duties differ because of the type of investment information they provide and the clients they work for. Financial analysts assess the economic performance of companies and industries for firms and institutions with money to invest. Personal financial advisors generally assess the financial needs of individuals, providing them a wide range of options.

FINANCIAL ANALYSTS

Financial analysts, also called securities analysts and investment analysts, work for banks, insurance companies, mutual and pension funds, securities firms, and other businesses, helping these companies or their clients make investment decisions. Financial analysts read company financial statements and analyze commodity prices, sales, costs, expenses, and tax rates in order to determine a company's value and project future earnings. They often meet with company officials to gain a better insight into a company's prospects and to determine the company's managerial effectiveness. Usually, financial analysts study an entire industry, assessing current trends in business practices, products, and industry competition. They must keep abreast of new regulations or policies that may affect the industry, as well as monitor the economy to determine its effect on earnings.

Financial analysts use spreadsheet and statistical software packages to analyze financial data, spot trends, and develop forecasts. On the basis of their results, they write reports and make presentations, usually making recommendations to buy or sell a particular investment or security. Senior analysts may actually make the decision to buy or sell for the company or client if they are the ones responsible for managing the assets. Other analysts use the data to measure the financial risks associated with making a particular investment decision.

Financial analysts in investment banking departments of securities or banking firms often work in teams, analyzing the future prospects of companies that want to sell shares to the public for the first time. They also ensure that the forms and written materials necessary for compliance with Securities and Exchange Commission regulations are accurate and complete. They may make presentations to prospective investors about the merits of investing in the new company. Financial analysts also work in mergers and acquisitions departments, preparing analyses on the costs and benefits of a proposed merger or takeover.

Some financial analysts, called ratings analysts, evaluate the ability of companies or governments that issue bonds to repay their debt. On the basis of their evaluation, a management team assigns a rating to a company's or government's bonds. Other financial analysts perform budget, cost, and credit analysis as part of their responsibilities.

Education and Training

A college education is required for financial analysts. Most companies require financial analysts to have at least a bachelor's degree in business administration, accounting, statistics, or finance. Course work in statistics, economics, and business is required, and knowledge of accounting policies and procedures, corporate budgeting, and financial analysis methods is recommended. A master of business administration is desirable. Advanced courses in options pricing or bond valuation and knowledge of risk management also are suggested.

Mathematical, computer, analytical, and problem-solving skills are essential qualifications for financial analysts. Good communication skills also are necessary, because these workers must present complex financial concepts and strategies in easy-to-understand language to clients and other professionals. Self-confidence, maturity, and the ability to work independently are important as well.

Financial analysts must be detail oriented, motivated to seek out obscure information, and familiar with the workings of the economy, tax laws, and money markets. Strong interpersonal skills and sales ability are crucial to the success of both financial analysts and personal financial advisors.

Financial analysts may advance by becoming portfolio managers or financial managers, directing the investment portfolios of their companies or of clients. Personal financial advisors who work in firms also may move into managerial positions, but most advisors advance by accumulating clients and managing more assets.

Certification. Although not required for financial analysts to practice, certification can enhance one's professional standing and is strongly recommended by many financial companies. Financial analysts may receive the title Chartered Financial Analyst (CFA), sponsored by the Association of Investment Management and Research. To qualify for CFA designation, applicants must hold a bachelor's degree, must have three years of work experience in a related field, and must pass a series of three examinations. The essay exams, administered once a year for three years, cover subjects such as accounting, economics, securities analysis, asset valuation, and portfolio management.

Job Outlook and Earnings

Employment of financial analysts is expected to increase between 10 and 20 percent through the year 2012. As the number of mutual funds and the amount of assets invested in the funds increase, mutual fund companies will need increased numbers of financial analysts to recommend which financial products the funds should buy or sell.

Financial analysts also will be needed in the investment banking field, where they help companies raise money and work on corporate mergers and acquisitions. However, growth in this area could be constrained by the implementation of pending reform proposals that call for investment firms to separate research from investment banking. Firms may try to contain the costs of reform by eliminating research jobs.

Demand for financial analysts in investment banking fluctuates because investment banking is sensitive to changes in the stock market. In addition, further consolidation in the financial services industry may eliminate some financial analyst positions, dampening overall employment growth somewhat. Competition is expected to be keen for these highly lucrative positions, with many more applicants than jobs.

Median annual earnings of financial analysts were $57,100 in 2002. The middle 50 percent earned between $43,660 and $76,620. The lowest 10 percent earned less than $34,570, and the highest 10 percent earned more than $108,060. Median annual earnings in the industries employing the largest numbers of financial analysts in 2002 were as follows:

Management of companies and enterprises	$60,670
Securities and commodity contracts intermediation and brokerage	58,540
Nondepository credit intermediation	51,700
Depository credit intermediation	51,570
Other financial investment activities	74,860

Many financial analysts receive a bonus in addition to their salary, and the bonus can add substantially to their earnings. Usually, the bonus is based on how well their predictions compare to the actual performance of a benchmark investment.

PERSONAL FINANCIAL ADVISORS

Personal financial advisors, also called financial planners or financial consultants, use their knowledge of investments, tax laws, and insurance to recommend financial options to individuals in accordance with their short-term and long-term goals. Some of the issues that planners address are retirement and estate planning, funding for college, and general investment options. While most planners offer advice on a wide range of topics, some specialize in areas such as retirement and estate planning or risk management.

An advisor's work begins with a consultation with the client, from whom the advisor obtains information on the client's finances and financial goals. The advisor then develops a comprehensive financial plan that identifies problem areas, makes recommendations for improvement, and selects appropriate investments compatible with the client's goals, attitude toward risk, and expectation or need for a return on the investment. Sometimes this plan is written, but more often it is in the form of verbal advice.

Financial advisors usually meet with established clients at least once a year to update them on potential investments and to determine whether the clients have been through any life changes—such as marriage, disability, or retirement—that might affect their financial goals. Financial advisors also answer questions from clients regarding changes in benefit plans or the consequences of a change in their job or career.

Some advisors buy and sell financial products, such as mutual funds or insurance, or refer clients to other companies for products and services— for example, the preparation of taxes or wills. A number of advisors take on the responsibility of managing the clients' investments for them.

Finding clients and building a customer base is one of the most important parts of a financial advisor's job. Referrals from satisfied clients are an important source of new business. Many advisors also contact potential clients by giving seminars or lectures or meet clients through business and social contacts.

Education and Training

A college degree is strongly preferred for personal financial advisors. Employers usually do not require a specific field of study for personal financial advisors, but a bachelor's degree in accounting, finance, economics, business, mathematics, or law provides good preparation for the occupation. Courses in investments, taxes, estate planning, and risk management also are helpful.

Programs in financial planning are becoming more widely available in colleges and universities. However, many financial planners enter the field after gaining experience working as accountants.

Certification. Personal financial advisors are not required to seek certification, but doing so can be a valuable career asset. Personal financial advisors may obtain the Certified Financial Planner credential, often referred to as CFP, demonstrating to potential customers that a planner has extensive training and competency in the area of financial planning. The CFP certification, issued by the Certified Financial Planner Board of Standards, Inc., requires relevant experience, completion of education requirements, passing a comprehensive examination, and adherence to an enforceable code of ethics.

Personal financial advisors may also obtain the Chartered Financial Consultant (ChFC) designation, issued by the American College in Bryn Mawr, Pennsylvania, which requires experience and the completion of an eight-course program of study. Both designations have a continuing education requirement.

The American Institute of Certified Public Accountants (AICPA) offers the designation of Personal Financial Specialist (PFS) to CPAs who specialize in personal financial planning. This designation can only be acquired by CPAs who are AICPA members, have at least three years of experience in planning, and pass a comprehensive and rigorous personal financial planning exam.

A license is not required to work as a personal financial advisor, but advisors who sell stocks, bonds, mutual funds, insurance, or real estate may need licenses to perform these additional services. Also, if legal advice is provided, a license to practice law may be required. Financial advisors who do not provide these additional services often refer clients to those qualified to provide them.

Job Outlook and Earnings

Employment of personal financial advisors is expected to increase between 21 and 35 percent through the year 2012. The rapid expansion of self-directed retirement plans, such as 401(k) plans, is expected to continue. As the number and complexity of investments rises, more individuals will look to financial advisors to help manage their money. Financial advisors who have either the CFP certification or ChFC designation are expected to have the best opportunities.

A generally better educated and wealthier population, coupled with the approaching retirement of the baby boomers, will add to the need for financial advisors. In addition, people are living longer and must plan to finance more years of retirement. The globalization of the securities markets will increase the need for analysts and advisors to help investors make financial choices.

Deregulation of the financial services industry is also expected to spur demand for financial analysts and personal financial advisors. Since 1999, banks, insurance companies, and brokerage firms have been allowed to broaden their financial services. Many firms are adding investment advice to their list of services and are expected to increase their hiring of personal financial advisors. Numerous banks are now entering the securities brokerage and investment banking fields and will increasingly need the skills of financial analysts in these areas.

Median annual earnings of personal financial advisors were $56,680 in 2002. The middle 50 percent earned between $36,180 and $100,540. Median annual earnings in the industries employing the largest number of personal financial advisors in 2002 were as follows:

Securities and commodities
    contracts intermediation and brokerage $68,110
Depository credit intermediation   51,030
Other financial investment activities   74,260

Personal financial advisors who work for financial services firms are generally paid a salary plus bonus. Advisors who work for financial planning firms or who are self-employed either charge hourly fees for their services or charge one set fee for a comprehensive plan, based on its complexity. Advisors who manage a client's assets usually charge a percentage of those assets. A majority of advisors receive commissions for financial products they sell, in addition to charging a fee.

CERTIFIED FINANCIAL PLANNER BOARD OF STANDARDS, INC.

The growth of the financial planning profession during the early 1980s created a demand for more training and education for financial planners. The Certified Financial Planner (CFP) Board was founded in 1985 as the International Board of Standards and Practices for Certified Financial Planners, Inc., (IBCFP) by the College for Financial Planning and the Institute of Certified Financial Planners (ICFP). The IBCFP became Certified Financial Planner Board of Standards, Inc. (CFP Board) in 1994. As a professional regulatory organization acting in the public interest by fostering professional standards in personal financial planning, CFP Board establishes and enforces education, examination, experience, and ethics requirements for holders of the CFP certificate.

The CFP Board offers the CFP Certification Examination for financial planners. The procedure for those interested in obtaining this certification is as follows.

Education Requirement

All applicants must complete a board-registered education program. There are currently more than 285 academic programs offered at colleges and universities throughout the United States, including credit and noncredit certificate programs and undergraduate and graduate degree programs. Many programs offer online courses and self-study options.

Apply for Challenge Status

Applicants holding the following degree or certificates may sit for the CFP Board exam:

- Certified Public Accountant (CPA)—inactive license acceptable
- Licensed attorney—inactive license acceptable
- Chartered Financial Analyst (CFA)
- Doctor of Business Administration (D.B.A.)
- Chartered Financial Consultant (ChFC)
- Ph.D. in business or economics
- Chartered Life Underwriter (CLU)

Beginning in January 2007, a bachelor's degree, in any field of study or program, will be required to obtain CFP certification. Applicants who do not intend to obtain a bachelor's degree must complete the entire certification process, including the education, examination, experience, and ethics requirements, by January 2007. Candidates for CFP certification should allow time for any possible retakes of the CFP Certification Examination, as well as adequate time to complete the rest of the certification process by this date.

Experience Requirement

At least three years of qualifying full-time work experience are required for certification. Qualifying experience includes work that can be categorized into one of the six primary elements of the personal financial planning process. Experience can be gained in a number of ways, including:

- The delivery of all, or of any portion, of the personal financial planning process to a client
- The direct support or supervision of individuals who deliver all, or any portion, of the personal financial planning process to a client
- Teaching all, or any portion, of the personal financial planning process

The CFP Certification Examination

The CFP Certification Examination tests applicants' ability to apply financial planning knowledge to client situations. The ten-hour exam is divided into three separate sessions. Because of the integrated nature of financial planning, however, each session may cover all topic areas. All questions are multiple choice, including those questions related to case problems.

The CFP Board maintains a list of review courses, offered by independent firms, designed to assist individuals in preparing for the CFP Certification Examination. A list of the approved courses is available at the CFP Board website (cfp.net).

SUGGESTED READING

Hallman, G. Victor, and Jerry S. Rosenbloom. *Personal Financial Planning.* 7th ed. Chicago: McGraw-Hill, 2003.

Kess, Sidney. *CCH Financial and Estate Planning Guide.* 13th ed. Riverwoods, IL: Commerce Clearing House, 2001.

Nissenbaum, Martin. *Ernst and Young's Personal Financial Planning Guide.* 5th ed. New York: Wiley, 2004.

CHAPTER

8

ACCOUNTING IN CANADA

Canada has a free-market economy with businesses ranging from small owner-operated enterprises to multinational corporations. Canada's economic development was historically based on the export of agricultural staples and on the production and export of natural resource products such as minerals and forest products. Canada now ranks as one of the top ten manufacturing nations of the world. Also, the service industry has expanded rapidly in the last two decades.

The government's economic and fiscal policy aims to sustain economic growth and job creation by promoting private-sector growth, reducing the size of government, and reducing government debt. The federal government has appointed a minister responsible for privatization, and it has been selling Crown corporations deemed no longer essential to meet public policy goals. Several companies have already been privatized, including Canadair, Canadian National Railway's trucking division, Fisheries Products International, and Air Canada.

Canada and the United States in many ways share a common business environment and a common approach to financial reporting. The underlying accounting principles used in the two countries are to a large extent highly compatible. There are some differences, due in part to differences in the legal and political systems. Generally, there is more codification of accounting principles from official standards-setting authorities in the United States than in Canada. As a result, United States principles frequently are absorbed in Canada and become part of generally accepted practice without necessarily being incorporated in a Canadian standard.

Three recognized accounting bodies in Canada are the Canadian Institute of Chartered Accountants (CICA), the Association of Certified General Accountants, and the Society of Management Accountants (SMA).

CHARTERED ACCOUNTANTS

North America's first professional corporation of Chartered Accountants (CA), now known as the Ordre des Comptables Agréés du Québec, was instituted in Quebec in 1880. The national organization for public accountants is the Canadian Institute of Chartered Accountants (CICA). The practice of public accountancy in Canada is licensed by each provincial government. In most provinces, this has been restricted to CAs. Approximately sixty-eight thousand CAs are members of the CICA.

The CICA could be compared to the AICPA in the United States. Members in good standing of any of the ten provincial or two territorial Institutes of Chartered Accountants are automatically members of the CICA. The responsibilities of the CICA are as follows:

- Accounting and auditing research, in both private and public sectors, including developing authoritative accounting and auditing standards
- Acting as liaison with the federal government, public and private agencies, and national organizations
- Expression of the profession's viewpoint on national matters of concern
- Publication of a professional journal and other publications
- National communications and public relations
- Representing the Canadian profession internationally

The CICA Handbook has evolved over time and contains the codified accounting principles of the CICA's Accounting Standards Committee. This handbook is the single most authoritative pronouncement on generally accepted accounting principles (GAAP) and reporting practices in Canada. Most corporate and securities legislation requires financial statements to be prepared in accordance with the requirements of the handbook.

The handbook has gained quasi-legal status as containing the formal accounting principles by means of recognition by securities administrators and federal and provincial legislation. Codification of GAAP in Canada is not as extensive as in the United States. The emphasis in Canada is on using professional judgment in determining what constitutes fair presentation or good practice. A practitioner could use CICA guidelines, research studies, published financial statements of the industry involved, authoritative Canadian literature, and literature of other countries that normally would emphasize U.S. pronouncements.

The duties and responsibilities left to the jurisdiction of the provincial institutes when licensing CAs are as follows:

- Education, training, and admission of new members
- Professional conduct and ethics, including discipline and investigation of complaints
- Acting as liaison with provincial governments, agencies, and other organizations
- Provincial public relations and community service programs

Becoming a Chartered Accountant

In general, there are five steps one must complete in order to become a Chartered Accountant (CA). The requirements, as outlined by the CICA, are as follows:

University degree. The university degree can be in any area or discipline; a business degree is not required. Many successful CAs have undergraduate degrees in arts, science, engineering, and other disciplines. Also, some jurisdictions allow degree exceptions for mature students.

Specified university courses. These courses can be completed during the undergraduate university degree, on a part-time basis during completion of practical experience requirements, or through certain recognized graduate programs.

Completion of a Provincial Institute/Ordre student professional program. These programs offer graduate-level courses to ensure that all candidates acquire the competencies they will need as a CA. Candidates must register with their Provincial Institute/Ordre while completing their practical experience requirements; programs are designed to complement on-the-job experience. This requirement can be fulfilled regionally as follows:

- Western Canada. Universities and Chartered Accountants School of Business.
- Ontario. Universities, Institute of Chartered Accountants, and Ontario School of Accountancy.
- Quebec. Universities and Ordre of Professional Education Programs.
- Atlantic Canada. Universities and the Atlantic School of Chartered Accountancy.

Practical experience with an approved training office. This requirement is designed to ensure that candidates learn to apply their knowledge to actual situations. Training offices approved by a Provincial Institute/Ordre are generally CA firms, offices of provincial or national Auditors General, or provincial or national departments of revenue.

The Uniform Final Examination (UFE). The UFE is a three-day evaluation in which candidates demonstrate their proficiency in the CA competencies. To pass the UFE, candidates must demonstrate that they have acquired the competencies required to begin a professional accounting career. The UFE is set by the CA profession's Board of Evaluators. It consists of three papers written over three days, one each day. In each paper, the candidate responds to simulations and business scenarios that represent the kinds of challenges faced by CAs. The first paper is a five-hour paper consisting of a single comprehensive business simulation; the second and third papers are four-hour papers, each consisting of two or more simulations. The UFE is administered annually, in September.

A general breakdown of the exam and the weight assigned to each component is:

Organizational effectiveness, control, and risk management	10–20 percent
Finance	10–20 percent
Taxation	10–20 percent
Assurance	20–30 percent
Performance measurement	20–30 percent
Information and information technology	10–20 percent

Naturally, not all who embark on a career in public accounting necessarily remain in the field, but every CA has had the experience of public practice, since a period of practical experience with an accounting firm is required before a person can become a CA. About half the CAs in Canada work in public practice.

The size of public accounting firms varies considerably, depending on the needs of the clients served. All the Big Four firms have offices in the major cities in Canada. In large cities it is not unusual for a firm to have more than a hundred staff members, while other firms and other locations may have as few as two or three in the office.

The Canada Business Corporations Act and most provincial corporations acts specify the corporate records that must be maintained. Generally, these include shareholders' records, minutes of meetings, resolutions of shareholders, the articles of incorporation, and adequate accounting records. The accounting records may be maintained in any form (looseleaf, microfilm, computer prepared) that is capable of reproducing required information in written form within a reasonable time.

Auditing

One of the main functions of the CA in public practice is that of auditor. Auditing is the examination of an organization's financial statements and reporting on whether they present its results fairly. The auditing function of CAs is becoming increasingly important as more people are relying on the independence and expertise of CAs in reporting on financial statements. The purpose of the statutory audit is not formally defined in the law. However, the CICA Handbook (sec. 5000.01) states:

> The objective of an audit of financial statements is to express an opinion (usually to the shareholders) on the fairness with which they present the financial position, results of operations and changes in financial position in accordance with generally accepted accounting principles, or in special circumstances another appropriate disclosed basis of accounting, consistently applied. Such an opinion is not an assurance as to the future viability of an enterprise nor an opinion as to the efficiency or effectiveness with which its operations, including internal control, have been conducted.

The following audited statements are required (with appropriate footnotes and schedules): balance sheet, income statement, statement of retained earnings, and statement of changes in financial position. The standard form of the auditor's report follows:

Auditor's Report

To the Shareholders of XYZ Company:

I have examined the balance sheet of XYZ Company as at December 31, 2005, and the statements of income, retained earnings, and changes in financial position for the year then ended. My examination was made in accordance with generally accepted auditing standards, and accordingly included such tests and other procedures as I considered necessary in the circumstances.

In my opinion, these financial statements present fairly the financial position of the company as at December 31, 2005, and the results of its operations and the changes in its financial position for the year then ended in accordance with generally accepted accounting principles applied on a basis consistent with that of the preceding year.

City _____ Signature _____
Chartered Accountants
Date _____

This standard form is required for companies incorporated under the Canada Business Corporations Act. A few provincial statutes require slightly different wording, although the substance of the wording is the same as that of the preceding report and the scope and nature of the audit is not affected.

A reservation in an auditor's report is made either when there is a departure from GAAP or when there has been a limitation in the scope of the audit that results in the auditor being unable to determine whether there is a departure from GAAP. The auditor should provide an explanation of the reasons for any reservation in the report.

Taxation

A CA in public practice may specialize in tax advice. The tax field has experienced dramatic growth recently as individuals and corporations increasingly call on CAs for expert advice due to the complexities of tax legislation.

The federal government introduced major tax reform provisions in 1987 involving a general lowering of income tax rates accompanied by a broadening of the tax base. Taxes are imposed in Canada by the federal, provincial, territorial, and municipal levels of government. The bulk of total government revenues in Canada is represented by the various taxes imposed by the federal government, which in turn makes tax-sharing payments and grants to all of the provincial, territorial, and municipal governments.

In Canada income taxes are imposed federally under the authority of the Income Tax Act and provincially under the authority of the income tax legislation of each of the various provinces. The Income Tax Act requires that proper books and records be maintained by all persons subject to its provisions, including corporations, partnerships, and sole proprietors.

Management Consulting Services

Management consulting is a growing public practice. The CA's unique blend of expert knowledge and practical experience is a solid foundation for facing the challenges and demands of the field. The consulting projects are varied and tailored to the individual needs of the clients. Canadian public accountants working as management consultants would perform similar kinds of projects as their counterparts in the United States (see Chapter 1).

As in the United States, CPAs can work not only in the public accounting area, but also in business education and government. CAs with expertise are sought after to fill a large variety of positions. In industry, many corporate controllers are CAs and participate in formulating financial and administrative policies of the company. A career as a CA frequently leads to such positions as vice president–finance or treasurer of a large corporation.

Table 8.1 shows the average salary figures for public accounting firms. The table has been excerpted from a report compiled by Robert Half International.

It should be noted that certification in an area, a law degree, or a master's degree may increase the salary figures by 10 to 15 percent. Salaries will also vary according to geographic location.

For more specific details about any aspect of becoming a CA, contact the individual provincial institute. Addresses are listed in Appendix D.

Table 8.1 Annual Compensation in Canadian Public Accounting Firms

PUBLIC ACCOUNTANTS–LARGE FIRMS

Experience/Title	2004	2005
To 1 year	$34,750–$42,750	$35,750–$43,750
1 to 3 years	40,250–50,750	43,250–53,750
Senior	52,250–62,500	54,750–64,500
Supervisor	59,000–72,250	63,750–76,500
Manager	67,500–106,500	71,750–112,250

PUBLIC ACCOUNTANTS–SMALL TO MEDIUM FIRMS

Experience/Title	2004	2005
To 1 year	$32,000–$39,500	$32,250–$40,000
1 to 3 years	34,500–46,500	36,750–48,000
Senior	43,500–55,250	46,000–58,000
Supervisor	54,000–70,250	55,000–71,000
Manager	62,750–89,000	65,750–90,750

ANALYSTS–LARGE FIRMS

Experience/Title	2004	2005
To 1 year	$32,000–$39,000	$33,750–$41,000
1 to 3 years	38,750–51,750	41,000–52,000
Senior	55,250–72,000	54,750–73,250
Manager	65,500–88,750	69,250–90,500

ANALYSTS–SMALL TO MEDIUM FIRMS

Experience/Title	2004	2005
To 1 year	$31,000–$36,250	$32,750–$39,750
1 to 3 years	37,250–46,500	38,750–49,500
Senior	47,500–62,500	48,500–62,750
Manager	54,750–77,500	57,500–81,250

Source: Robert Half International, Inc., *2005 Salary Guide* (Canadian version). Used by permission.

CERTIFIED GENERAL ACCOUNTANTS

In the early 1900s, Montreal was the financial and economic center of Canada. The demand for trained accountants was growing, especially among large corporations. John Leslie, controller and vice president of Canadian Pacific Railway, helped form the Canadian Accountants' Society in 1908 for the purpose of helping personnel within his organization upgrade their accounting skills and their careers. Five years later the group received its federal charter and the right to set standards and examinations across Canada and to grant the designation Certified General Accountant (CGA).

The association enjoyed steady though modest growth until the 1950s. It was at this time that the group saw the need for a new type of accounting education program, one that would allow students to continue working and earning a living as they studied for their professional designation.

There are now active CGA associations in every province and territory. Today, membership in the Certified General Accountants Association (CGA) has grown to 62,000.

CGAs work throughout the world in industry, commerce, finance, government, public practice and other areas where accounting and financial management is required. CGA clients range from major corporations and industries to entrepreneurs. Their expertise is valued in the public sector, government, and the corporate world.

A major purpose of the CGA organization is to provide and maintain a uniform educational program of high quality. To accomplish this, the CGA has established its Program of Professional Studies, a competency-based program designed to ensure that CGAs possess the following skills:

- Professional expertise in accounting and related areas
- Effective communication, management, and leadership skills
- Interpretive, judgmental, and analytical skills
- Competence in the use of the computer as a management and accounting tool
- Management of change in the technologies, processes, and structures of organizations
- Use of complex information systems in decision making

All candidates for CGA certification must complete practical work experience and assessments. In general, thirty-six months of approved work experience are required; however, a candidate may be judged acceptable after an assessment at twenty-four months.

The CGA program consists of a combination of eighteen academic course and exam requirements that may be satisfied by CGA examinations or by transfer credits from postsecondary study. Candidates must also pass four Professional Admission Comprehensive Examinations.

The Program of Professional Studies consists of the following levels:

Foundation Studies

Level 1

Financial Accounting 1

Economics 1

Law 1

Computer Tutorials

Level 2

Financial Accounting 2

Quantitative Methods 1

Management Accounting 1

Communications 1

Level 3

Financial Accounting 3

Finance 1

Management Information Systems 1

Business Case 1

Advanced Studies

Level 4

Management Accounting 2

Accounting Theory 1

Auditing 1

Taxation 1

Business Case 2

Completion of the above courses is followed by the Professional Admission Comprehensive Exams (PACE). Candidates select one of the following four areas, each of which includes four examinations: corporate and small/medium enterprise; information technology; government and not-for-profit; or public practice.

Complete information about CGA certification is available on the CGA website at cga-online.org.

THE SOCIETY OF MANAGEMENT ACCOUNTANTS

The Certified Management Accountant (CMA) program was established to provide accountants in management in private firms with an alternative to the CA program. This is not to imply that an accountant cannot obtain both certifications.

In order to gain the CMA designation, a candidate must complete a university degree that includes courses in the following areas:

Management Studies
Management accounting
Corporate finance
Operations management
Information technology
Strategic management
International business
Human resources
Marketing

General Accounting Studies
Financial accounting
Taxation
Internal control

Related Studies
Economics
Commercial law
Statistics

Candidates next take the Entrance Examination, which tests accounting and management knowledge. The exam consists of two parts, each administered over four hours. Part 1 is a multiple-choice exam; part 2 is a complex business case. The exam is divided into two categories weighted as follows:

General accounting studies   33 percent
Management studies   67 percent

The Entrance Examination is given twice each year, in June and October.

After passing the Entrance Examination, candidates begin the Strategic Leadership Program. This two-year program is simultaneous with full-time employment and is designed to expand on the knowledge gained through on-the-job training. The program consists of six learning modules and a final business case that is presented to a panel of CMAs.

Practical experience is considered to be an essential component of the accreditation process. The integration of on-the-job experience with professional program studies helps candidates develop management skills and assures employers that a CMA possesses competency in the application of management principles and accounting knowledge. The practical experience requirement consists of two levels of experience: operational and managerial. All candidates for the CMA designation are required to complete twenty-four months of practical work experience, preferably running concurrently with the Strategic Leadership Program.

The salary figures in Table 8.2 for various corporate financial positions have been excerpted from a report compiled by Robert Half International, Inc. It should be noted that certification in an area, a law degree, or a master's degree may increase the salary figures by 10 to 15 percent. Salaries will also vary according to geographic location.

Most CMAs are employed in industry, and the field of concentration has been in cost and management accounting. Regulatory legislation in Ontario, Quebec, Newfoundland, Nova Scotia, and Prince Edward Island restricts the practice of public accounting by CMAs. For more information on the specific requirements necessary in a province or territory, refer to addresses in Appendix D.

GOVERNMENT ACCOUNTING

There are some significant differences between the U.S. and Canadian systems of government. The major distinctions are as follows:

- Canada functions under a parliamentary system. Funding and policy decisions are made almost entirely in the executive branch by the Prime Minister and Cabinet.
- Canada has only about one-tenth the population of the United States, and its central government is proportionately smaller.

Table 8.2 Corporate Financial Salaries in Canada

CFOS/TREASURERS

Company $ Volume in Millions	2004	2005
50–100	$87,250–$123,250	$91,750–$130,500
100–250	104,250–150,750	113,500–158,000
250+	139,000–239,000	150,750–250,750

CONTROLLERS–CORPORATE

Company $ Volume in Millions	2004	2005
0–50	$66,000–$90,000	$66,250–$90,750
50–100	69,750–97,750	69,250–98,750
100–250	83,250–121,500	84,250–122,250
250+	92,250–144,750	96,000–146,500

ASSISTANT CONTROLLER/TREASURER

Company $ Volume in Millions	2004	2005
0–50	$54,000–$75,500	$54,750–$73,250
50–100	61,500–80,250	61,250–80,500
100–250	62,250–88,000	68,250–91,500
250+	80,000–110,000	80,500–109,250

TAX MANAGERS–CORPORATE

Company $ Volume in Millions	2004	2005
50–250	$78,500–$109,000	$82,250–$112,000
250+	104,000–155,000	107,000–159,250

Source: Robert Half International, Inc., *2005 Salary Guide* (Canadian version). Used by permission.

- Canada has much clearer separation in functions between the central and provincial governments than exists between the federal and state governments in the United States.

The information in Table 8.3 shows average salaries for bookkeeping and payroll clerks.

Table 8.3 Bookkeeper and Payroll Salaries in Canada

BOOKKEEPERS

Title	2004	2005
Accounting Clerk	$25,250–$34,500	$27,250–$35,250
Bookkeeper/Assistant	30,250–38,750	32,000–38,500
Full Charge	36,000–46,250	38,500–45,500
Accounts Receivable/ Payable Supervisor	38,750–54,250	40,500–56,250

PAYROLL

Title	2004	2005
Administrator	$29,750–$36,000	$30,000–$35,250
Coordinator	33,750–43,750	43,750–53,750
Supervisor	42,750–54,500	43,750–53,750
Manager	48,250–65,250	48,500–74,250

Source: Robert Half International, Inc., *2005 Salary Guide* (Canadian version). Used by permission.

Auditor General

The watchdog over the government's fiscal activity in Canada is the Office of the Auditor General (OAG), which is much like the Government Accountability Office (GAO) in the United States. Traditionally, the Auditor General's Office examined departmental performance and expenditure control by focusing on isolated examples of improprieties discovered during field audits. To provide Parliament with a better understanding of the underlying problems, the Auditor General has adopted a more comprehensive departmentalized systems-based approach. The departmentwide audits concentrate on the following areas:

- Financial controls
- Attest function
- Management controls
- Electronic data processing

The OAG issues only one report a year to Parliament. It contains the results of several of these comprehensive audits as well as chapters on the office's other major activities.

The Comptroller General

The Office of Comptroller General (OCG), established in 1978, is an agency in the Canadian government's executive branch. The responsibilities of the OCG include:

- To oversee the quality and integrity of financial systems and related practices
- To develop and maintain policies, procedures, and practices necessary to evaluate and report on the efficiency and effectiveness of government programs

The OCG establishes government-wide policies on program evaluation and internal audit activities in the executive departments. Individual departments and agencies are encouraged to conduct their own evaluation of the effectiveness and efficiency of their programs, with guidance from the OCG.

In the area of internal audits, the OCG publishes government-wide standards similar to the GAO's yellow book. Canada's internal auditors perform roles similar to those of the GAO's inspectors general.

Canada Revenue Agency

Federal and provincial tax legislation is administered by the Canada Revenue Agency (CRA). The CRA administers tax laws for the government of Canada and for most provinces and territories. It also administers various social and economic benefit and incentive programs delivered through the tax system. The main office of the CRA is located in Ottawa, the nation's capital, with district offices located throughout the country.

The department is the responsibility of the Minister of National Revenue, but the day-to-day operations of the income tax branch of the department are under the general direction of the Deputy Minister of National Revenue for Taxation, who is a senior public servant.

In Canada, income taxes are imposed federally under the authority of the Income Tax Act and provincially under the authority of the income tax legislation of the various provinces. Most provincial income taxes are administered and collected by the federal government.

For additional information on government jobs in Canada, visit the CRA website at cra-arc.gc.ca/careers.

ACCOUNTING EDUCATOR

In Canada, as in the United States, the main function of the accounting faculty member at an accredited university is to present an in-depth study of the field of accounting. The faculty member usually specializes in one area of accounting, such as financial, managerial, tax, auditing, and not-for-profit organizations. Some Canadian universities have a separate accounting department; others have accounting faculty within the College of Business or, commonly, the accounting faculty is part of the Faculty of Management. Chapter 6 describes general information on the accounting educator.

THE FUTURE

Demand for accounting clerks and bookkeepers is increasing due to economic expansion that has resulted in more financial transactions. The anticipated rate of growth for the occupation is above average. In addition, companies will need to fill jobs left vacant by retiring workers.

For financial auditors and accountants, the rate of employment growth will likely be below average, but demand should increase somewhat because organizations are expected to need more analysis of business operations and sophisticated accounting systems. The number of retiring workers should contribute to job openings. Successful candidates will need a good understanding of technology as well as the ability to use accounting and auditing software. The ability to analyze business operations and to offer management and consulting services will also lead to greater job opportunities.

The employment growth rate for financial managers will likely be above average because of ongoing business trends such as the globalization of markets, corporate mergers/acquisitions, and the increasing complexity of financial transactions. It is expected that the number of job openings will exceed the number of job seekers, making this a good area for opportunities. Necessary skills include a firm knowledge of technology and information systems as well as financial reporting and management systems.

SUGGESTED READING

Information is available from organizations responsible for licensing and certifying accountants in Canada (see Appendix D).

C H A P T E R

9

ACCOUNTING TRENDS TODAY

Many accountants are movers and shakers in a fast-paced business world that belies the staid reputation of the profession. Some of them are corporate chief financial officers (CFOs) or treasurers. Others are IRS investigators and FBI agents. They must keep up with all the latest business trends. Through ongoing education, accountants are monitoring key trends such as new computer technology and globalization of business, trends that will vitally affect their career success.

ACCOUNTING AND AMERICAN BUSINESS

Accountants must be proficient in numeracy, the mathematical equivalent of literacy. In today's fast-paced and rapidly changing business world, a new level of numeracy is required.

Facility with numbers is the first order of business for accounting students, and in today's world of commerce, ability to manipulate numbers via online spreadsheets is also a given.

In addition to purely computational skills, accountants must demonstrate superior analytical reasoning when faced with business problems in consulting engagements. In fact, many accounting educators stress courses that require students to write and reason in order to prepare for the consulting work they will need to do with clients.

Ethical awareness is also vital in a profession that deals with money and its temptations daily. An accounting firm's reputation is entirely based on its maintenance of high ethical standards, which are developed and publicized in the United States by the industry's professional associations. These standards are in addition to the legal requirements and regulations of the nation's business law.

Career tracks for accountants in the changing structure of business may take several diverging paths. One traditional path leads through the ranks of a company's financial department, or more likely, through a succession of jobs with different companies, advancing higher in the ranks through accountant, tax manager, assistant controller, toward the CFO position. Another leads to partner in a public accounting firm, after many years as junior and senior accountant.

Entry-level jobs may mean junior accountant or a management-level job in the financial division, depending on the background of the student when he or she enters the job market. More important than job title is career path: it is important to get on the right track to begin with if you want to make partner in an accounting firm; if you're aiming for CFO of a corporation, that's a different track. Before making your course selection take some time for critical career planning, which will contribute to your success in today's competitive job market.

EDUCATION FOR TODAY'S ACCOUNTING CAREERS

Students with an accounting interest can consider several options for higher education. If your immediate goal is an entry-level job with a small investment of time and tuition, it may be enough to enroll in a two-year college program for accounting technicians such as those offered at some community or state colleges. However, to get the most career-boosting potential from your education, complete the four-year college bachelor's degree program as soon as possible. A bachelor's degree in liberal arts (with an economics major, for example) could be paired with an M.B.A. or master's of accounting later on to build a solid foundation for career advancement.

Getting this education is a tall order. First you must get accepted at the college of your choice and figure out how to finance the cost of college, tuition, lodging, and meals (see Chapter 10 for information on financial aid). In the United States, graduation, plus job experience and a CPA, are the next hurdles.

There has been a dramatic expansion in the body of accounting knowledge over the last decade. Significant increases in official accounting and auditing pronouncements and the proliferation of new tax laws are two factors that have expanded the knowledge base that professional practice in accounting requires. In addition, mergers and acquisitions, combined with the corporate accounting scandals of the late 1990s, have also contributed to the changes in regulations and controls imposed on accountants.

If the profession is to respond positively to the development of new technologies and to society's demand for expanded information, it needs to have broadly educated individuals who are technically knowledgeable and who have the analytical abilities, communication and interpersonal skills, and the cultural awareness that will enable the profession to fill its broader role.

In response to these changes, the membership of the AICPA voted to make 150 semester hours of education a requirement for new members of the organization after the year 2000. As of March 2005, forty-five states have adopted the 150-hour requirement; the remaining five are in the process of doing so.

The AICPA has made recommendations for ways in which students can fulfill the 150-hour requirement. A master's degree is not a must, since students can meet the requirement at the undergraduate level or get a bachelor's degree and take some courses at the graduate level. The following options are also available:

- Combine an undergraduate accounting degree with a master's degree at the same school or at a different one.
- Combine an undergraduate degree in some other discipline with a master's in accounting or an M.B.A. with a concentration in accounting.
- Enroll in an integrated five-year professional accounting school or program leading to a master's degree in accounting.

In most cases, however, the additional academic work needed to acquire the technical competence and develop the skills required by today's CPA is best obtained at the graduate level. Graduates of master's programs are better equipped to combine technical knowledge with the required skills in communication, presentation, and interpersonal relations needed by successful CPAs.

In addition, studies have shown that students who have a maser's degree have a substantially higher rate of success on the Uniform CPA Examination. Further, master's degree holders receive starting salaries that are approximately 10 to 20 percent higher than the starting salaries of those with only bachelor's degrees. Finally, there is evidence that promotions to manager and partner and to corporate managerial positions are increasingly going to individuals with master's degrees.

In light of these positive statistics, professional organizations such as the AICPA, the National Association of State Boards of Accountancy, and the Federation of Schools of Accountancy have consistently supported the 150-hour education requirement for entry into the accounting profession.

And learning doesn't stop there. Tax accountants monitor changing tax codes through continuing education programs; financial accountants need to learn about new debt instruments or securities; management accountants brush up on the latest software for decision support and analysis. Education becomes a lifelong pursuit.

Many academic institutions offer advanced degree programs in accounting specialties; the flow of information and education through other sources such as associations and private business seminars is constant. In the United States, the AICPA offers accountants three options for career development through certificate programs: a tax planning and advising course sequence, a personal financial planning program (see Chapter 7), and a business valuation certificate. In Canada, the Canadian Institute of Chartered Accountants expanded its range of educational courses in response to high demand that in some courses—such as a specialized tax course called Wealth Preservation—filled classrooms to overflowing. The CGA now includes information technology as a category in its program of studies, reflecting the integration of accounting and information systems in the business world.

Increasingly, education doesn't end at graduation. It continues through academic institutions, consulting firms, and nonprofit associations, among others, that are available to accountants at all stages of their careers.

COMPUTERS IN ACCOUNTING

Computer skills are essential for advancement in all of these jobs. Industry observers agree that technology is probably the biggest single factor changing the profession today and expect computers and technology to continue to change the profession.

Many bookkeeping tasks are done by data processing systems. Write-up work goes faster online. Again, computer knowledge is a critical factor for companies that are trying to do business overseas, and an accounting firm that knows financial software can offer a key service to customers.

Today's students are well equipped to handle the computer requirements that are fast becoming part of the accounting profession, having grown comfortable with computers, using e-mail, news groups, blogs, and search engines with greater ease than their predecessors. This ability will help both in studies and in a career as an accountant.

Beyond that, accountants must know the software that's widely used in their field. Almost every business will have some kind of accounting information system (AIS). It may be as simple as a commercial, low-end software package. If clients are small businesses, they may automate with this off-the-shelf software that gives them basic integrated accounting capabilities. The accountant must know how to navigate inside applications like Quicken, QuickBooks, Money, or Peachtree Accounting. These and others will become familiar fast if clients are in the $1 million to $5 million range or smaller. Bigger clients need more accounting power and use a different type of software, such as Solomon IV or Microsoft Great Plains, to name just two of the brands on the market.

All these applications take the tried-and-true accounting tools, such as the general ledger, journal, accounts receivable, accounts payable, and inventory, and replicate these tools in a computerized environment.

Opportunities are plentiful for accountants with a solid knowledge of AIS technology. In the book *Core Concepts of Accounting Information*, Nancy A. Bagranoff and her colleagues write,

> Students taking courses in AISs often wonder if there are special career opportunities combining the study of accounting with computer science and information systems. The answer is that almost endless employment opportunities await such graduates. Accounting employers are very interested in hiring students who have emphasized information systems in their study of accounting. This means that the traditional jobs in accounting are available to those who study AISs in addition to other career opportunities that you may never have considered.[1]

INTERNATIONAL OPPORTUNITIES

In a global economy, an American-trained accountant can be a valued employee anywhere in the world. If you're inclined toward international finance and marketing, as are many M.B.A. graduates, you can choose from a wider array of job options than your stateside colleagues.

Accounting firms have always searched far and wide for clients. They have enjoyed the dynamic and sometimes turbulent world of business and taken pride in their own technical prowess at accounting.

Consider the following excerpt from the diaries of Edwin Waterhouse, written over one hundred years ago. In his memoirs Edwin Waterhouse (of the founding family of PricewaterhouseCoopers) tells how he got one account during a business trip to Ireland in 1886:

> Before the month of November was over I again crossed to Larne by the pretty Stranraer route—this time in the interests of the Belfast and Northern Countries Railway. A question had arisen at the board as to whether some expenditure should be treated as capital or revenue outlay; and I was requested to examine into the accounts and report. I went down on the night of the 30th and was back in London on the 3rd December, staying the night of the 2nd at the house of the chairman of the company, the Rt. Hon. John Young of Galgorm Castle, Ballymena, about one hour distant by rail from Belfast. I was much interested in the old house, adapted as a residence from one of the old castles of refuge of a more turbulent age.
>
> Before I left I pointed out to Mr. Stewart, the secretary, a weak point in the company's methods of account keeping; so also an apparent inaccuracy to which I thought the attention of the company's auditors ought to be called. Soon after my return I learnt that the accountant and cashier had thought it fit to make themselves scarce, and that extensive frauds upon the company had been discovered. I was asked to suggest a new and reliable accountant and had the pleasure of recommending a Mr. Bailey of the South Eastern [Railway] offices, a gentleman of whose abilities we had formed a high opinion. He became a very useful official of the Irish company. The accounts were carefully examined into and reported on by Price, Waterhouse & Co. and subsequently audited by them half yearly; and the business of the company under the chairmanship of Mr. Young steadily improved.[2]

The scale of enterprise far outdistances the economies of the nineteenth century. The global market that is forming now could multiply such stories a thousandfold. The steamship and railway era of "around the world in eighty days" has been replaced by the speed of light and the time reduced to nanoseconds in which financial information can cross international borders. There are those who predict a coming together of world economies to agree on international accounting standards.

Internationalization of Accounting Standards

Some experts divide the world into four accounting models or systems: the British-American-Dutch model, the Continental model, the South American model, and the communist model.[3] The legal systems and the business structure of the countries within each system tend to be the same or similar.

The British-American-Dutch model uses the same basic accounting principles as the United States, and is shared by North America, Australia, and India. The system is designed to serve the needs of investors and an active legal system.

The Continental model includes the European countries and Japan, and accountants here focus on the information needed by government authorities. The economies here rely more on banks for business capital.

The South American model suits the needs of government planners and sets rules for businesses. This system has had to adapt to periodic inflation in economies of its countries.

The communist model, which is less widely used since the changes in the economies of Russia and the Commonwealth of Independent States after 1993, contained accounting rules that served the requirements of government planners in centrally controlled economies.[4]

To add one more piece to this round-the-world tour of accounting systems, consider the developing countries. International standards would help them to establish accounting systems as well as provide more opportunities for the far-ranging corporations and firms of established economies.

Will a universal accounting standard ever be established? The International Accounting Standards Committee (IASC) Foundation is working toward that goal. The IASC was founded in June 1973 as a result of an agreement by accountancy bodies in Australia, Canada, France, Germany, Japan, Mexico, the Netherlands, the United Kingdom and Ireland, and the

United States, and these countries constituted the Board of IASC at that time. The IASC operated from 1973 until 2001, when the International Accounting Standards Board (IASB) assumed accounting standard-setting responsibilities.

The IASC is the parent entity that oversees the IASB. The International Accounting Standards Board is an independent, privately funded accounting standard-setter based in London. The Board members come from nine countries and have a variety of functional backgrounds. The IASB is committed to developing, in the public interest, a single set of high-quality, understandable, and enforceable global accounting standards that require transparent and comparable information in general purpose financial statements. In addition, the IASB cooperates with national accounting standard-setters to achieve convergence in accounting standards around the world.

When it does happen, international standardization will simplify the work of many international businesses and speed the globalization of commerce.

Crossing Borders

Crossing just one border can complicate a corporation's life as well as improve its fortunes. A well-known example that has appeared in more than one textbook and in the *Journal of Accounting Case Research* is the financial history of baseball's Toronto Bluejays, who pioneered the internationalization of major-league baseball. In the 1980s, on the verge of a world championship and planning a brand new—and expensive—home at the Toronto SkyDome, to be funded by public and private sources, the Bluejays were facing a financial squeeze play, along with their business partners in the stadium construction project. With a new stadium to pay for and a huge payroll, the team's front office needed a financial home run. One creative tactic: exploit the currency differences between Canadian dollars and U.S. dollars to hedge in financial markets. The team may have saved millions that way. Another tactic: use the domed stadium for convention business attracted north from U.S. cities such as Boston; finally, sell the stadium to a consortium of investors in the private sector. To play baseball today, you need world-class financial accounting talent!

In multinational firms the situation becomes even more complex. International corporations need accountants who can sort out the tax laws of the dozens of countries where they do business. They also need financial acumen to anticipate the consequences of their company's business moves.

For example, consider the implications of FASB Statement No. 109 "Accounting for Income Taxes." Under this standard, deferred income taxes have to be adjusted "to reflect changes in tax rates made from time to time by taxing authorities in the jurisdiction in which the company operates." Let's say that a company has customers not only in the United States, Europe, and Japan, but in emerging markets in Asia and Latin America. If the company also targets markets such as China, India, Brazil, and Colombia, its financial officers must rationalize policies to show the best results after taxes in dozens of nations. In this context FASB 109 becomes a tall order, as adjustments are made not just for changes in U.S. law, but for all countries in which the company does business. It falls to the financial executives to deal with interactions of several countries' currency factors and tax laws in calculating the best business strategy for the company.

Because business crosses international boundaries to find the areas of greatest opportunity, many companies and even countries want to participate. The Big Four firms routinely advise clients about this. One of the most exciting opportunities for top accounting graduates is to join a multinational team to do such work.

In what may be one of the most far-reaching developments in the world of business and accounting, the banking system of China has been modernized over the last decade to keep pace with the growth of Chinese industry and Asian trade. Several big international accounting firms have been heavily involved, acting in a consulting role. Western accounting groups from the United States, Canada, and other countries have also been involved in training a new generation of China's businesspeople.

Cracking the Global Marketplace

The Big Four firms dominate the international scene, routinely auditing the U.S. Fortune 500 firms and many of the largest overseas firms. However, second-tier accounting firms and even local firms have found opportunities in advising smaller companies on import and export business and the tax effects of operating overseas. The challenges for auditors are found in tasks like monitoring foreign exchange rates, watching cash flow from multiple sources, and linking diverse computer systems together, in addition to concern about marketing, travel, and personnel.

There's a major opportunity for small companies that crack the global marketplace, too, and these companies usually don't have the advice of a

Big Four firm. However, they still need the same help as larger companies to get through the maze of international laws and regulations safely. In addition to taxation, such small companies might seek the advice of accountants about their capital needs, setting up foreign offices, choosing financial software, or developing a strategic plan that has the financial horsepower to succeed. The U.S. government is actively pushing such companies into the world arena in an effort to create jobs and help the economy grow.

It has been suggested that mid-sized accounting firms can position themselves to serve this growing need. The training that goes into this requires special attention to international laws and regulations, beyond the foundational accounting education, but it is a niche that may prove rewarding to accountants of the twenty-first century, who will be doing business worldwide.

NOTES

1. Nancy A. Bagranoff, Mark G. Simkin, and Carolyn Strand Norman, *Core Concepts of Accounting Information Systems*, 9th ed. (New York: John Wiley & Sons, 2004).
2. *Memoirs of Edwin Waterhouse*, ed. E. Jones (London: B. T. Batsford, 1998), 118.
3. Jamie Pratt cites Gerhard Mueller, H. Gernon, and G. Meek, *Accounting: An International Perspective* (Homewood, IL: Irwin, 1987) as the source of this descriptive model.
4. Jamie Pratt, *Financial Accounting in an Economic Context* (Cincinnati, OH: South-Western Publishing, 1997), 26–27.

SUGGESTED READING

Books

Bagranoff, Nancy A., Mark G. Simkin, and Carolyn Strand Norman. *Core Concepts of Accounting Information Systems*. 9th ed. New York: John Wiley & Sons, 2004.

Boynton, William C., Raymond N. Johnson, and Walter G. Kell. *Modern Auditing*. 7th ed. New York: Wiley, 2001.

Horngren, Charles T., Gary L. Sundem, and William O. Stratton. *Introduction to Management Accounting*. 17th ed. Englewood Cliffs, NJ: Prentice Hall, 2004.

Inside the Minds Staff (eds.). *Inside the Minds: Leading Accountants: CEOs and Practice Group Leaders from Ernst & Young, KMPG, BDO Seidman and More on the Future of the Accounting Industry and Profession.* Boston: Aspatore Books, 2001.

Jones, Edgar (ed.). *The Memoirs of Edwin Waterhouse: A Founder of Price Waterhouse.* North Pomfret, VT: Trafalgar Square Publishing, 1988.

Pratt, Jamie. *Financial Accounting in an Economic Context.* 6th ed. New York: John Wiley & Sons, 2005.

Stickney, Clyde, and Roman L. Weil. *Financial Accounting, an Introduction to Concepts, Methods, and Uses.* 10th ed. Cincinnati: South-Western College Publications, 2002.

Other Sources

For more information on the international scope of accounting, see the websites of the Big Four accounting firms (see list at the end of Chapter 1) or of accounting organizations such as the Institute of Management Accountants, American Institute of CPAs, or Canadian Institute of Chartered Accountants (see Appendixes).

C H A P T E R 10

GETTING STARTED ON A CAREER

How will you finance your education? In what area of accounting do you want to work? What do you expect to be doing in three years? In five years? In ten years? These are easier questions to ask than they are to answer. Setting goals will help you establish guidelines when deciding on a career.

SETTING GOALS

It is never too early or too late to learn how to set goals. A student in high school or one starting college should be familiar with the process and use it for career planning, and should know how to separate wishing from planning when setting those goals.

Business organizations are looking for people who can develop and implement their goals. The process of developing clearly stated goals involves brainstorming, thinking, refining, and ranking. It is important to have a clear picture of your goals, rather than a vague idea of what you think you want to accomplish. They should be stated in specific language so you know when a particular goal has been achieved. Writing the goals down makes them easier to remember, update, and revise. Examples of vague goals and how to make them more specific are shown in Table 10.1.

An important part of goal setting is to remember that it is acceptable for goals to change. In fact, it is necessary for your goals to be updated as you grow professionally.

Table 10.1 Vague and Specific Goals

Vague Goal	Specific Goal
Get a job	Be hired by a Big Four firm next year *or* Be hired as a cost accountant for XYZ Corporation
Make more money	Earn $40,000 next year
Continue education	Graduate with a master's degree in 2007 *or* Pass CPA exam next year
Get ahead in life	Be a manager in three years *or* Start own accounting practice in five years
Travel more	Make specific plans to travel to England for two weeks next year

Goals should be established for long and short time frames. Drawing a time line (Table 10.2) and placing personal and professional goals on it will aid you in determining whether certain goals are compatible and in proper sequence.

Activities that will help accomplish the desired goal should be listed. An example of a goal and some suggested related activities leading to the accomplishment of that goal are shown in Table 10.3.

FINANCIAL AID OPPORTUNITIES

The old saying "it takes money to make money" comes to mind when talking about the cost of a good education to launch a career in accounting. Fortunately, there are many sources of funds. The federal government's loan programs are divided into three types of loans: Stafford loans, Perkins

Table 10.2 Time Line for Specific Goals

3 Years	6 Years	10 Years
Graduate from college	Senior accountant in tax department	Partner in accounting firm
Obtain job with Big Four accounting firm		

Table 10.3 Desired Goal and Related Activities

Goal: To obtain entry-level position with a Big Four accounting firm or with XYZ Corporation after graduating from college.

ACTIVITIES

Finance college education

Join Beta Alpha Psi

Participate in an internship program

Learn to prepare a résumé

Learn to write a cover letter

Plan for an initial interview

Plan for the office interview

loans, and PLUS loans (loans for parents). There are other types of money available from the government, such as consolidation loans and Federal Supplemental Educational Opportunity grants (FSEOGs). Be sure to ask about them; but remember, they are more specialized loans with limited applicability. In addition to loans, the government offers outright grants through the Pell Grant program. These grants to qualifying students do not have to be repaid. To determine if someone is eligible, the Department of Education uses a standard formula set by Congress.

Stafford Loans

The Stafford loan program is available to both undergraduates and graduate students. Current ceilings on loan amounts for dependent undergraduates are $2,625 for the first-year or freshman student (interest rates are currently 7.66 percent, with a ten-year term).

An independent student is eligible for $2,625 in subsidized loans plus $4,000 in unsubsidized loan funds. Subsidized means you don't have to pay any interest until after you graduate. The loan is repaid after graduation and a grace period, and deferrals are possible. The interest rate can change annually on July 1. It is tied to U.S. treasury bill interest rates, but under current law it can't exceed 8.25 percent interest for the balance of the loan term.

Stafford loans carry a fee of up to 4 percent of the loan, deducted proportionately from each loan disbursement. Because of this deduction, you'll receive slightly less than the amount you're borrowing.

After completing one year of studies, the student can borrow up to $3,500 for a dependent undergrad, on a subsidized basis; unsubsidized loans of $4,000 are available to eligible independent students. A junior or senior can borrow slightly more, currently $5,500 subsidized, and independent students can qualify for up to $5,000 in additional unsubsidized loans.

A graduate student can borrow up to $8,500 subsidized and $10,000 unsubsidized. The upper limit on total Stafford loans to a graduate or professional school student currently is $65,500 in subsidized and $63,000 in unsubsidized funds. The limit on total debt from all Stafford loans is currently set at $46,000 for qualified undergraduates and $138,500 for graduate students.

Perkins Loans

The Perkins Loan program was set up to serve students in financial need. A Perkins loan is a low-interest-rate loan currently offered at a 5 percent rate. It's open to both undergraduates and graduate students. The student's school determines need based on family finances and contributions to education. The federal government provides each participating school with a certain amount of Perkins funds each year. Once these funds are dispersed, no additional monies are available for that year. Therefore, it is advisable to submit an application for a Perkins loan as early as possible.

For an undergraduate, credit lines run up to $4,000 a year and top out at a ceiling of $20,000. A graduate student, however, can receive as much as $6,000 each year up to a total of $40,000 (including undergraduate loans). The loan has to be repaid in ten years. Typically, it's paid back on a monthly installment plan after graduation.

Direct PLUS Loans

A newer addition to the government loan program is the Direct PLUS Loan, available through the Federal Family Education Loan (FFEL) Program. There is no limit on these loans. The loan amount is calculated based on your total need less any loans you already have. If a student has a $6,000 need, for example, and $2,000 is taken care of by other loans, he or she can get up to $4,000. The only requirement is for the parents to pass a credit check. The school furnishes applications. The interest rate could change each year of repayment but does not exceed 9 percent. For July 1, 2002, to June 30, 2003, the interest rate for PLUS loans in repayment was 4.86 percent. Interest rates are adjusted each year on July 1.

Taking the Plunge

Taking a loan is a big responsibility. The student (and parents) should be sure all loan terms are well understood before closing on the loan. Some time-tested advice from various sources follows.

Before you enroll in a college program, talk to your school counselor about financial aid. Talk to family friends who've gone through the whole process. There are many sources of aid. When you've gathered the latest information on programs you qualify for, compare them carefully to find the best aid package: the lowest interest rate (or blended rate if you have two or more loans) and a flexible repayment schedule.

Given the seriousness of financing a college education, many people are intimidated by the financial aid application process and put off filing until the last possible minute. This can lead to errors that might reduce your loan amount. It is always a good idea to review the applications thoroughly to be sure that you have all the required information. All colleges and most high schools offer assistance for students and parents who are completing financial aid applications; take advantage of any available expert advice and submit your applications as early as you possibly can.

How to Apply

For the U.S. Department of Education loan programs (the Stafford Loan, Perkins, Direct PLUS), you must complete the Free Application for Federal Student Aid (FAFSA) form. This form is available through the financial aid offices of most colleges and high schools, or on the web at fafsa.ed.gov. The website provides complete information about filing deadlines, required documentation and signatures, as well as a pre-application worksheet. In addition to the FAFSA, all applicants must sign a promissory note, which is a legal document indicating your agreement to repay the loan as specified by the lender. Your money will come from the government directly to the school or the lender and then to you. If you're applying based on financial need, you don't have to start paying the loan back immediately; you can arrange for a deferred payment plan. Otherwise, the loan payments with interest begin as soon as you get the money. To qualify, you have to be a full-time or half-time student in a qualified program and meet certain other requirements.

Other Sources of Funds

If the terms of the government loans don't suit you, look into other sources of funds, private as well as public. Scholarships for your field, from your local schools or community organizations, and various national educational organizations (National Merit Scholarships and others) are worth a try. Many scholarships are available for students who are members of certain minority or ethnic groups. Some professionals and executives are entitled to tuition reimbursement for dependent children. Your state is also a source of scholarship funds.

Lenders now have programs designed for college-bound students and their families, though interest is charged at market rates, not subsidized as are the government's. Still, lenders may be competitive on the basis of loan term (a home equity loan, for example, can be stretched out over twenty years, versus the government's ten-year term).

Rates and loan terms change frequently, and federal funding is subject to budget constraints and congressional approval, so be sure to get the latest information before deciding on an aid package. You're going to be an accountant, so you'll want to figure out the best loan package for you!

ENHANCING YOUR COLLEGE EDUCATION

Once you have settled the financial aspects of your education, it is time to take additional steps to make the most of your accounting studies.

Joining Beta Alpha Psi

Beta Alpha Psi is an international honorary organization for students and professionals in the field of financial information, which includes accounting, finance, and information systems.

There are local chapters at over 250 colleges throughout the United States and internationally. Requirements for membership vary from college to college, but generally include maintaining a specified grade point average, attendance at meetings, community service, and payment of dues.

Usually at least two meetings are held each month throughout the regular academic school year. Students, faculty, and persons from the community employed in various areas of financial information attend. At professional meetings speakers discuss topics of interest to students, including such items as interviewing practices, local employment outlook, computers, and auditing.

Social meetings may find a company's employees playing a volleyball game against the students, competing at bowling, or enjoying a picnic. A formal induction into the club is held in conjunction with a banquet for both fall and spring terms of school.

Tours of local accounting firms and business offices are arranged during which students can observe office facilities and employees. These tours give students a chance to see work environments and ask questions.

The advantages of joining Beta Alpha Psi are the interaction with people employed in various areas of accounting and financial information and the prestige of being a member of an honorary fraternity in one's chosen field. Membership in Beta Alpha Psi will enhance your chances of getting a job in accounting.

Participating in an Accounting Internship

An accounting internship program is a cooperative program between a college and a public accounting firm, corporation, or government agency. An accounting senior or second-semester junior may work full- or part-time for ten to fifteen weeks as a member of a professional accounting staff performing entry-level accounting assignments. Students obtain academic credit for the work (ranging from two to twelve credits). The student usually returns to the university for one or more terms of study after completing the internship. An alternative to the internship program is a cooperative education program (co-op). A co-op program usually involves at least two separate sessions at the same company or firm, with the student alternating school terms with the work experience.

Before students decide on a program, they should talk to various companies and firms to determine the right internship program for them and to decide if the potential delay of graduation for one academic term is worth the experience. Some companies prepare brochures describing their internship programs, while others send representatives to the campus to explain their particular programs.

Annual publications such as *Internships 2005* (Peterson's Internships) and *The Princeton Review's Internship Bible* are valuable resources. Internships may be advertised in campus newspapers and advertised on college campuses through placement offices, on billboards, through faculty members, campus newspapers, and books. Many professional associations offer information on internships available with member companies. Visit the websites of associations listed throughout this book for more information.

An internship or co-op program can be beneficial to students by giving them an opportunity to obtain valuable on-the-job training before graduation. A student has the chance to apply accounting concepts and theory already learned in the classroom to practical job-related situations. These experiences cannot be simulated in textbooks or classrooms. There will be many opportunities for an intern to use good judgment, show responsibility and technical ability, demonstrate a cooperative attitude, and communicate with others. Learning the routine of an eight-to-five job is a different experience for many college students.

Interns who accept an assignment become paid members of the company's professional staff. Compensation levels are normally standardized within a university's internship program and generally average about 75 percent of the entry-level salary. The company usually pays no fringe benefits, such as vacation or insurance. At many of the companies and firms, the interns are compensated for overtime hours, but often at the straight-time pay scale.

Depending on the company or firm, an intern may either be reviewed weekly or at the completion of each major job assignment. At the end of the internship, the performance review will be discussed and formalized as part of the exit interview. A copy will usually be sent to the intern coordinator at the college. General areas where the intern's performance will be rated include:

- Knowledge of accounting
- Ability to follow instructions
- Accuracy in performing tasks
- Tact and interpersonal skills
- Willingness to cooperate

- Appearance
- Punctuality
- Communication

A successful internship or co-op program often leads to a job offer with the firm or company. It gives the student valuable experience and aids in the student's future decision about what accounting areas to consider for a career.

Any student interested in an internship or co-op program should discuss the alternatives with an accounting teacher or chairman of the accounting department to become familiar with any specific requirements or filing deadlines.

JOB SEARCH SKILLS

In addition to your accounting education, you will need some specific skills aimed at helping you to get an interview and find a job.

Preparing a Résumé

A good résumé can and should open doors for you. A résumé is a selling document, and its major purpose is to persuade the reader to grant you an interview. While it is standard practice to send copies of the same résumé to several different companies, it is advisable to write a different résumé for each type of job sought. The résumé written for a job in public accounting, for example, would have a different job objective than a résumé targeted to a corporate job.

Résumés that get results usually include a specific job objective, a section showing experience for the job, and a detailed but concise description of education, special honors, and awards. Keep in mind that a résumé should be no longer than one page, especially for someone who is fairly new to the job market.

It is suggested that any work experience related to the position desired be listed before education. Everyone applying for the job will have an educational background quite similar to yours, so it is very important to stress any experience that relates to the job. For example, if you have worked in the accounts payable division of a company for summer employment, a line in the experience section of the résumé might read, "Handled and expedited invoices from suppliers." A student who participated in an internship or co-op program would include that information in this section. The key to describing your experience is to use action verbs that indicate management functions. Action verbs that are commonly used on résumés include such words as *advised, communicated, controlled, created, generated, implemented, managed, negotiated, surveyed*, and *trained*.

In the education section, name the college you attended and year of graduation, and list all degrees you received. Mention your cumulative grade point average only if it is 3.0 or higher. List all of your academic honors and special achievements. Include any special seminars or courses you have taken beyond the required courses in your field of study. List your membership in Beta Alpha Psi or an accounting club.

Personal data, including marital status, height, weight, age, health, race, and number of children should not be listed on the résumé, because the Equal Employment Opportunity Law prohibits such factors from being used as a basis for discrimination in hiring.

At the end of the résumé, include the statement, "References will be provided upon request." Do not list the names of your references on the résumé itself. It is important to spend some time deciding whom to use as references. You should ask one or two of your professors for a letter of recommendation. Professors should be provided with more information about you than they have from classroom interaction alone. Try to provide this additional information at the time you ask a professor to give you a reference. Use an employer as one of your references if possible.

There are various types of résumés that are suited to different experience levels. Be sure to choose the format that most closely fits your education and experience.

• Chronological résumé. This format lists education and work experience chronologically, starting with the most recent. The chronological résumé is well suited to a job seeker who is following a career path in which one job leads naturally to the next.

• Functional résumé. This résumé format is appropriate for those who are applying to a specific company in the hope that a position is available for which they are qualified. In a functional résumé, you can include experience, classes taken, and any other information that pertains to the job you are interested in, listed under individual headings.

• Digital résumé. Many employers now require the digital submission of résumés, due in large part to the high volume of résumés received by most companies. There are two types of digital résumés. Electronic résumés are sent by e-mail or posted to a website. Scannable résumés can be read by a computer. An electronic résumé can be sent to a specific employer by e-mail or submitted to an online job search site such as Monster.com or CareerBuilder.com. Some companies use technology to scan and store résumés in a database, which can then be scanned for keywords and phrases that match the job descriptions. There are specific rules for preparing both types of digital résumés. Most of the job search websites offer résumé preparation guidance. Your college library or guidance center should have books on the topic as well.

Writing a Cover Letter

Each résumé sent should be accompanied by an individual cover letter, addressed to a specific person within the company, using the person's full name and title. The letter should stress what you feel you can contribute to the operations and goals of the particular company. If possible, study the company's annual report. Most college libraries have reference materials that can be used to provide current information on specific companies. The Dun & Bradstreet Directories (dnb.com), Moody's Investor Services (moodys.com), and Thomas's Register (thomasnet.com) all provide specific company information, such as the contact information, what the business produces, its annual sales, and the names of officers and directors.

Reading professional journals and publications such as *Fortune*, *BusinessWeek*, and the *Wall Street Journal* is another way to gain information about different companies and the successful employees who hold key positions.

Be sure that your cover letter and résumé include all of your contact information. If you give a cell phone number or e-mail address, be sure to check your messages regularly so as not to miss a response from a potential employer.

Planning for an Initial Interview

The placement office at many colleges provides opportunities for firms and companies to interview students at the college. The traditional times for scheduled interviews are October and May. The employers give the placement office specific days when they will be on campus, and the students sign up for short interviews (usually a half-hour maximum). Many students sign up for an interview with more than one firm or company. The college requires the student to complete a placement file including a transcript, résumé, and personnel sheet before he or she is allowed to participate in the interview process.

Following are some of the questions asked frequently by interviewers:

- What is your major strength?
- What do you regard as your outstanding qualities?
- What is your major weakness?
- Tell me about yourself.
- Why did you choose this college?
- Why did you choose accounting as a major?
- What did you like best about college? About your last job?
- What did you like least in college? In your last job?
- What contributions could you make to the company?
- In what way does this job meet your career goals and objectives?
- What are your long-range goals and objectives?
- What kind of position would you like to hold in five years? In ten years?

An interviewer is not going to ask you every one of these questions, but these are some of the more common ones; therefore, it is important to take some time before the interview to formulate some answers to these questions and individualize them for your own needs. A person should present the best possible picture at the interview. Turn any negatively phrased question into something positive. For example, if you are asked, "What did you like least about college?" you might respond, "I was frustrated that time constraints prevented me from taking extra courses."

Planning for the Office Interview

A student will usually learn the results of this initial interview within two weeks. A positive response from a firm or company normally includes an invitation to visit the office for a half- or full-day interview. This will include an opportunity to visit with three or more company employees, a tour of the office, and lunch.

You will be asked questions and will be observed during the visit. A decision on whether to hire you will be made by the employees who meet you. You may accept an office visit from more than one firm and may receive offers of permanent employment from more than one firm. It is at this point that you must make a decision.

Appearance

Your physical appearance plays an important part in molding your image. You can do a great deal to control your image if you are concerned with the type of impression you make when meeting someone for the first time. This is crucial during an interview. Observe others' reactions to you. It is important for you to have a formal education, but it is equally important to be knowledgeable in the art of image building.

Well-dressed people inspire confidence and assure those with whom they are doing business that they are trustworthy, knowledgeable, and have the client's interest at heart. As an accounting professional, you are representing your employer as well as yourself when you meet a client or any other member of the public. Professionals have many roles, and clothes can help them handle those roles better. Clothing is one of the variables almost completely within your control.

If you are still in college, you may find literature from various firms helpful. Information on different firms is available in the college library or placement office, or it may be obtained by writing to individual firms. The acceptable dress code is not usually listed in a firm's brochure, but photographs of the employees are included, and much information can be obtained by observing what the employees are wearing. (For a list of Big Four firms and the addresses of their national headquarters, see Chapter 1.)

At many colleges, students are invited and encouraged to attend some of the meetings sponsored by the state CPA societies, the National Association of Accountants, and the American Society for Women Accountants. If you attend these meetings, you can observe what practicing accountants are wearing. Naturally, clothing styles and colors may vary from city to city.

If you know practicing accountants in industry, education, government, or public accounting, it is acceptable to ask them for guidance in the area of proper dress.

Clothes are an investment in the future, and they are important to a professional in his or her career. Your clothes should be an expression of the kind of person you are—or of the person you hope to be. Career clothing is designed to deliver a certain message. Your message should say, "I'm here for my accounting future, and I expect to go far in my chosen profession."

Your Complete Package

When looking for a job that will lead to a rewarding career, a student must present a complete package. Your academic performance, experience in related areas, and extracurricular activities, as well as the ability to dress and communicate in a professional manner, all enter into the selection process.

Extracurricular activities can be rewarding and also help you achieve recognition. For example, regional meetings for the American Accounting Association (AAA) present opportunities for students to submit research papers on various topics in accounting. Awards are given for the best paper at the graduate and undergraduate levels. The recipients are recognized at a luncheon or dinner meeting, and their papers are included in the material received by all registrants. Meetings are held periodically at different locations in many states. The chairman of the department of accounting has information available about these types of opportunities.

A worthwhile activity to consider while you are in college is tutoring other students in accounting. This will strengthen your accounting knowledge and helps portray you as a contributing, interested student to the faculty and potential employers. At some universities this may be done on a volunteer basis; other universities may offer paid tutoring jobs.

SUGGESTED READING

Cassidy, Daniel J. *The Scholarship Book 11th Edition: The Complete Guide to Private-Sector Scholarships, Fellowships, Grants, and Loans.* Upper Saddle River, NJ: Prentice Hall Press, 2004.

College Board. *College Cost & Financial Aid Handbook 2005: All-New 25th Edition.* New York: The College Board, 2004.

CHAPTER 11

MAXIMIZING YOUR CAREER

Completing college and getting the desired job in accounting are important goals, and when they are achieved, you should be congratulated. Your next step is to be successful on the job. The goal "to be successful" should be defined in specific and measurable ways if it is to be useful. For example, "I expect to be promoted to senior tax accountant within eighteen months" allows for measurable and quantifiable results.

Some of the personal techniques you will need to be successful on the job include:

- Being organized
- Communicating
- Maintaining a career-oriented attitude
- Being assertive
- Using power
- Finding a mentor
- Networking
- Promoting yourself

BEING ORGANIZED

Being organized implies being in control, and control starts with planning. Proper planning means bringing the future into the present so you can do something about it now. Planning and making choices are hard work.

It may appear as though you have little free choice. Of course, there are constraints on everyone that make totally free choice impossible: health, age, education, and present job conditions. It is up to the individual, however, to make choices in the areas where there is the possibility of choice. For example, part of your work will include completing certain assigned tasks:

- Finish a departmental budget report by four o'clock
- Interview two candidates for a cashier position
- Evaluate alternatives for a more efficient method of processing the payroll

You have no choice but to complete these projects. As part of your planning process, you can make a list and set priorities on activities that need to be done to accomplish these tasks. Which of these tasks is more important? Which ones have to be completed first? What activities can be delegated? These are some of the questions that need answers in the planning stage. Working on them is the first step in gaining control of your work.

Your planning should apply both to your personal and to your professional life. There is no quick, easy way to gain control of your time and your life. Getting started is the first step, then you must practice setting goals, listing activities, and prioritizing them until this process becomes routine. This will make you much more efficient and organized.

COMMUNICATING

Communication is the process of delivering a message, written or oral. It involves the transmission of the ideas and images of one person or group to another individual or group. The secret of good communication is to have the receiver understand the message the way the sender meant it to be understood.

Written Communication
One of the primary ways of communicating with others is through writing; in fact, effective writing is one of the most important job skills. Employers are often aware of writing deficiencies in many of their employ-

ees, and some firms offer seminars to train their people to be more effective writers. It is widely recognized that writing effectively leads first to communicating effectively and ultimately to managing more effectively.

The following are basic principles for effective and efficient business writing:

- Use brief, simple, and direct wording
- Make a reader want to cooperate
- Avoid technical jargon and clichés

The business letter. Major advantages of written communication are its permanent record, relative formality, and capacity to convey complex ideas. The disadvantages include high cost, low speed, and lack of immediate feedback.

Words have personality. Some create a vivid, sharp image, and others show action or mood. Skilled writers develop a sensitivity to words and strive for those that produce the desired effect.

Every field of study or organization develops its own jargon, which eventually evolves into an everyday vocabulary for the people who use it. If there is any doubt that your reader will understand your specialized language, use laypeople's terms. Avoid clichés and cluttered phrases. Words that add nothing to the meaning of the sentence should be deleted.

The effectiveness of a letter depends on the organizing of sentences into logical paragraphs. Because people prefer to receive information in manageable chunks, most paragraphs should be kept short. A common rule of thumb states that sentences should be kept under twenty words and paragraphs should be fewer than one hundred words. Paragraphs should have a topic sentence that expresses the main idea. The topic sentence conveys more emphasis if placed at the beginning or end of the paragraph instead of being buried in the middle.

Every business letter satisfies the following two functions: it attempts to convey a message and it projects an image of its writer. The style will leave an impression of both you and your employer. Your letter should be kept as simple as possible while still conveying the proper meaning. It is very important that clients interpret the information in the manner you intend it.

The memorandum. Memos serve a useful purpose but should be used sparingly. Many of the guidelines suggested for the business letter also apply to the memo. A memo conveys written messages within an organization.

Some of the significant differences between a letter and a memo are that the memo is less formal, the sender and receiver of the message probably know each other, and the memo should deal with only one subject.

E-mail. Virtually all business workers today communicate by e-mail, whether with coworkers or clients. By its nature, e-mail is intended to quickly relate a brief message and is useful in business for many purposes. It saves time and money when communicating long-distance, giving e-mail an advantage over the telephone or mail. Although it is less formal than a business letter or memorandum, e-mail used in a business setting is still officially a form of written communication. It is important to remember, however, that like other forms of writing, your e-mail style also reflects your professionalism. Do not use abbreviations or symbols; spell out all words and use proper capitalization and punctuation.

Oral Communication

Most people spend a part of every day talking with others. It may be a casual, unplanned conversation as two people meet in an office corridor. At a chance meeting, a person should be pleasant and use good grammar. An exchange might be a simple "hello" or might involve mentioning a current event or a topic of interest about the company.

The speech is a more formal method of communication. When giving a speech, it is very important to know the subject well. Do research on the topic if necessary. As you gather statistics, documents, reports, or other information, keep in mind the type of audience who will be listening. A talk on tax shelters should not be delivered to the general public in the same manner as it would to a group of practicing CPAs.

The presentation should be concise, whether given to three or thirty or three hundred people. A talk should have three parts: an introduction that tells what one is going to say, the body in which it is said, and the conclusion in which one summarizes what was said. In other words, keep your speech simple and reinforce the main points. Your presentation should be compact in format. Be careful not to add "ah," "uh," or "um" as fillers. There is nothing wrong with a slight silent pause. In fact, sometimes it can be an attention-getter.

Act interested in the subject and the audience. Smile occasionally and try to look relaxed. Eye contact is important—do not scan the crowd but look at one individual for several seconds and then move on to someone else. This gives the audience the feeling that you are interested in them as individuals and keeps them interested in you and your topic.

Some people prefer to write the entire speech out because they are afraid they will forget what to say when they are in front of a group. If a speech is written out, care must be taken when it is presented not to sound as though it is being read. Some prefer to rehearse a speech four or five times before giving it and then time it. You can use note cards listing only brief key phrases in case you need to refer to them. This makes the speech more spontaneous but still lets you feel prepared.

Your tone of voice is important because it informs and persuades and because it expresses your feelings about yourself and other people. Your voice can project self-assurance or insecurity, interest or indifference, happiness or depression.

A tape recorder can be a useful tool to help you monitor your voice. Practice an important speech by recording it, playing back the tape, and noting the areas that need improvement. If done properly, the same speech may be delivered to a handful of people or to hundreds with the same positive results.

Suppose an accounting manager wants to convince the budget committee that her department's budget for the next fiscal year is justified. The budget does not have as good a chance of being accepted if the manager is not an effective speaker. Of course, other factors in her presentation are equally important and will influence the final decision: the way she is dressed, her overall presence and preparedness, and the reasonableness of the budget.

Visual aids have become an integral part of many presentations. They can reinforce the major points and concepts of a talk. These aids can range from a simple flip chart to a PowerPoint presentation to slides with a sound track. Each aid should be planned and coordinated to fit smoothly into the talk. Effectiveness is weakened if too much information is displayed at one time.

Nonverbal Communication

In addition to written and oral communication, you communicate nonverbally. Your body language delivers messages, too. Some body movements have either positive or negative effects on viewers. As a professional, make sure your body language is sending the message you want people to receive.

Sometimes body language betrays a person by conveying messages that are in conflict with the spoken word. An employee tells his superior how happy and excited he is about his new promotion to cost accounting manager. If he is slumping, slouching, sitting with his elbows on the table, or with his chin in his hand, the message is probably not being received as intended.

What does facial expression reveal? It can and should enhance one's power and effectiveness. If you are expressing acceptance, you should not be scowling; if anger, you should not be smiling; and if interest in another person's conversation, you should not have a blank, bored look.

Remember, looking and acting with poise is important for a professional and can do much for one's image. How a man or woman acts usually has more impact than what he or she says. Objective information is revealed by the language used, but your body conveys how you feel about what you are saying. Whenever there is a discrepancy, the nonverbal message is likely to be taken as the true meaning.

Listening Skills

For most people, listening is not a skill that is easy to develop. Listening may be considered as an opportunity to gather needed information. You can prevent some misunderstandings, mistakes, and bad working relationships by listening carefully. Good listening requires a conscientious effort and a sense of balance—there is a fine line between gaining needed company knowledge and hearing someone's troubles and complaints.

MAINTAINING A CAREER-ORIENTED ATTITUDE

How do you make your employer realize you think you have a career at XYZ Company and not merely a job? Act like a professional. Be willing to travel and accept overtime if that is routine practice in the office. Certification in one of the areas of accounting is important. (See Chapters 1 and 2 for further discussion of certification.) Willingness to attend training sessions or seminars to increase your knowledge is important. These usually include skill-building topics or current updates of technical information. Many seminars give the accountant continuing professional education (CPE) credits. CPE credits are needed in most states to keep various certifications current. Training sessions or seminars are usually paid for by the employer.

Obtaining a master's in business administration or a master's in accountancy may be very worthwhile. It could increase your salary and give you a better chance for promotion while also letting the employer know you are serious about your career. Most companies pay part or all of the tuition for their employees.

College accounting teachers are expected to publish articles or books and to conduct research as part of their jobs. They are also expected to participate in university activities and to be involved in their community. By fulfilling these requirements, accounting educators show that they are serious about their career. In whatever area accountants are employed, they must convince management or the administration that they are an integral part of the team.

BEING ASSERTIVE

In today's business environment, competition is considered a way of life. Planning to win requires a "game plan." It means that you must use the environment to your advantage. Often, competition is associated with aggressive behavior, which implies getting your own way regardless of the consequences to others. For many people the word *aggressive* connotes negative feelings. Aggression may be more palatable if it is referred to as self-initiative.

Today, psychologists are teaching people it is better and healthier to be assertive than it is to be aggressive. Assertive behavior allows you to describe your thoughts and feelings without attacking or blaming another person. In this way assertiveness differs from aggressiveness.

As an assertive person, you will come to recognize the importance of behavioral changes, including changes in your thoughts, feelings, attitudes, and usual ways of handling problems. Because assertion is a very personal learning experience, it is necessary for you to examine your own particular needs.

Assertive behavior has positive consequences. When you assert yourself, you feel more in control of your life and experiences. This is a personal power that does not come at the expense of someone else or of a relationship.

You will have many opportunities to be assertive. Everyone experiences criticism on the job, at least occasionally. If it is realistic, helpful criticism, the assertive person responds by acknowledging that the criticism is valid. If the problem lies in you, and you are working on the problem and trying to modify your behavior patterns, you should state that fact. If you are receiving criticism and have been unaware that a problem existed, you can ask for help or suggestions on ways to correct the situation. If you are giving criticism, be careful to avoid aggression. If aggressive behavior is used to criticize someone, the person receiving the criticism probably will become angry or defensive. This does not result in any productive behavior modification or change.

USING POWER

Competing in a fair manner and being assertive help an accounting professional develop a sense of power in the corporate organization. Power is defined as the ability to influence another person and to get another person to think, feel, or do something. Power has more than one source. In the article "The Bases of Social Power," the authors define five types of power[1]:

1. Reward power. The power to give or withhold something that is perceived as being valuable to another person.
2. Coercive power. The power to inflict some kind of punishment that the other person wants to avoid.
3. Legitimate power. The power to exert authority legitimately, to use the influence of one's title or of one's position.
4. Referent power. The power that other people give us because they respect us, like us, approve of us, or are attracted to us.
5. Expertise power. The power that other people give us because of our special knowledge and competence.

Almost all people use one or more of these power sources when they try to influence others. Reward and coercive power have rather direct results in a business setting: reward power in the ability to give a raise or promotion, and coercive power in the power to fire or demote an employee. Legitimate power is exhibited when a memo is issued from the director of internal auditing to all subordinates that there is a meeting at 2:00 P.M. and their attendance is expected, or when the director of budgeting states that all budgets will be finalized and handed in by May 18 at 5:00 P.M.

Referent and expertise power are not automatically given. They must be earned by displaying competency, self-confidence, self-assurance, control, and intelligence. These two kinds of power are harder to achieve and do not always equate with job status. A controller is not necessarily given referent or expertise power just because he or she has achieved that level in the organization.

FINDING A MENTOR

A mentor is a teacher who can instruct and guide you as a protégé. If you choose a mentor wisely, he or she will influence your career, sometimes dramatically. Traditionally, the mentor is considered someone two or more levels higher than the protégé in the organizational structure.

When you first join the company, your mentor may be a peer or someone lower in the organization (perhaps a secretary). This mentor's purpose is to show you the ropes, giving practical information about the office and the people in it. Be sure that the advice you are receiving is correct. This relationship may not last long; its main purpose is to gain initial information.

Whom do you pick for a mentor? A potential mentor should be someone you like and someone with whom you are compatible. He or she should be someone in a position to influence your career, someone who is a leader in your company. The characteristics of successful leaders vary. There is no one profile; however, there are a few key characteristics that most leaders have in common[2]:

- A strong ego
- A high level of energy
- A high level of intelligence
- The ability to conceptualize
- The ability to make decisions
- The ability to communicate well
- The ability to relate to others

How do you make a potential mentor notice you? If you have determined someone is a potential mentor, you should already know some of his or her likes and dislikes, some of his or her hobbies and habits. If you know the person is interested in a particular author, you might cut out a review of this author's latest book and send it to the mentor with a note asking, "Do you agree with this review?" Find out what business organization he or she belongs to. Join if you are eligible, or ask him or her for sponsorship. Ask the person's advice on a career or business-oriented decision. All of these ideas will get your potential mentor's attention. It may take a year or more to cement a mentor relationship, and remember, not every potential relationship one tries to establish will work.

If one is fortunate to establish a successful mentor-protégé relationship, it may last for five or ten years or longer. As a mentor is promoted in the company, his or her power to help the protégé becomes even greater.

One of the dangers of this relationship becomes apparent when the mentor suffers a political reversal within the company. In such cases, the effects are also felt by the protégé. Another problem is not knowing when or how to release yourself from one mentor and move on. Usually, close emotional bonds have been established that are hard to loosen.

Someone who has experienced being a protégé in a mentor-protégé relationship feels an obligation to assist younger people early in their careers. The rewards are great!

NETWORKING

In geometry there is a theorem that states that the whole is equal to the sum of its parts. In networking theory, the whole is greater than the sum of its parts. Networking is a way of gathering information, obtaining referrals or assistance from group members, and gaining contacts. In some ways, networking has the same effect as a chain letter; as one meets more people, the number of possible contacts increases.

Networking can be accomplished in groups that are formal or informal, structured or unstructured. With informal networking there may be no regular meetings. This type of network is possible with neighbors or with people in your department or on the same floor at work. Networking is very important for a sole practitioner or anyone working in a management position in a public accounting firm. New clients are gained through referrals from present clients or from direct contact with the accountant. These contacts may be made at a country club, tennis club, or athletic club, as well as in more structured settings.

A more structured form of networking can be achieved by joining a professional organization. Most of the professional organizations have local, state, and national groups or affiliates. Advantages of structured, formal networking are educational seminars and meetings, interaction with professionals with similar problems and aspirations, and a chance to expand your circle of contacts. (See Appendix A for a list of professional accounting organizations and their addresses.)

A cost accountant might choose to join the local chapter of the National Association of Accountants, which emphasizes managerial accounting. A member of the internal audit staff could join the Institute of Internal Auditing. Any certified public accountant (CPA) could join the local chapter of the state society of CPAs.

Building networks is exciting and interesting. A person has the opportunity of becoming acquainted with people, never knowing when that contact might be used in a positive way.

PROMOTING YOURSELF

Many people believe if they study hard, perfect their accounting skills, and do their jobs well, they will be recognized, given more opportunities, and promoted. They believe that merit has its own rewards. This is just not true.

The fact that the budget is done on time and the financial statements balance at the end of each month is not enough. Fulfilling the job description is not enough. Employers expect quality work; that's what you are paid for. If you do nothing to promote skills and competency, you may be overlooked.

On the job, keep a file of any activities you have performed that go beyond the job description. If a suggestion or idea sounds worthwhile, write a memo about it to the boss. It could be a suggestion on updating a section of the internal control manual or a new approach on credit collection procedures, for example.

Involvement in community service, giving a speech, or doing other volunteer work, even if it is not directly related to the job, should be noted and publicized when possible. When you give a lecture to a group of businesspeople on the changes in a new tax law, or present a program to high school students informing them on careers in accounting, send a news release to the local paper. Most city papers include a business page or section. If space permits the item will be published and you will have free publicity. Make sure activities are also printed in the company or university newsletter.

If you do it assertively, promoting yourself need not appear obnoxious or offensive. Positive self-presentation is crucial for the professional accountant. If you think you are a worthwhile, interesting person, other people will be convinced too. You will be considered a winner—and isn't that what it is all about?

NOTES

1. J. R. P. French and B. Ravin, "The Bases of Social Power," in *Group Dynamics*, 2nd ed., eds. D. Cartwright and A. F. Zander (New York: Harper & Row, 1960), 607–623.
2. Linda Phillips-Jones, *The New Mentors and Proteges: How to Succeed with the New Mentoring Partnerships* (Grass Valley, CA: Coalition of Counseling Centers, 2001).

SUGGESTED READING

Dobson, Michael Singer, and Deborah Singer Dobson. *Enlightened Office Politics.* New York: American Management Association, 2001.

Griffin, Gerry, and Ciaran Parker. *The Games Companies Play: An Insider's Guide to Surviving and Winning in Office Politics.* Mankato, MN: Capstone Press, 2002.

McIntyre, Marie G. *Secrets to Winning at Office Politics: How to Achieve Your Goals and Increase Your Influence at Work.* New York: St. Martin's Griffin, 2005.

Satterfield, Mark. *Power Prospecting.* Irving, TX: Mandalay Press, 2002.

Tullier, Michelle. *The Unofficial Guide to Landing a Job.* New York: Wiley, 2005.

APPENDIX

NATIONAL ACCOUNTING-RELATED ORGANIZATIONS

American Accounting Association
5717 Bessie Drive
Sarasota, FL 34233
aaahq.org

American Institute of Certified
    Public Accountants
1211 Avenue of the Americas
New York, NY 10036
aicpa.org

American Society of Women
    Accountants
8405 Greensboro Drive, Suite 800
McLean, VA 22102
aswa.org

American Taxation Association
aaahq.org

American Woman's Society of
    Certified Public Accountants
136 S. Keowee Street
Dayton, OH 45402
awscpa.org

Association of Government
    Accountants
2200 Mt. Vernon Avenue
Alexandria, VA 22301
agacgfm.org

Association of Public Treasurers of
    the U.S. and Canada
962 Wayne Avenue, Suite 910
Silver Spring, MD 20910
aptusc.org

Beta Alpha Psi
1200 Avenue of the Americas, 19th
    Floor
New York, NY 10036
bap.org

Information Systems Audit and
  Control Association
3701 Algonquin Road, Suite 1010
Rolling Meadows, IL 60008
isaca.org

Financial Executives International
200 Campus Drive
Florham Park, NJ 07932
fei.org

Government Finance Officers
  Association of the United States
  and Canada
203 N. LaSalle Street, Suite 2700
Chicago, IL 60601
gfoa.org

Healthcare Financial Management
  Association
Two Westbrook Corporate Center,
  Suite 700
Westchester, IL 60154
hfma.org

Institute of Internal Auditors
247 Maitland Avenue
Altamonte Springs, FL 32701
theiia.org

Institute of Management
  Accountants
Ten Paragon Drive
Montvale, NJ 07645
imanet.org

National Association of Black
  Accountants
7249-A Hanover Parkway
Greenbelt, MD 20770
nabainc.org

National Association of College
  and University Business Officers
2501 M Street NW, Suite 400
Washington, DC 20037
nacubo.org

National Association of State
  Auditors, Comptrollers, and
  Treasurers
2401 Regency Road, Suite 302
Lexington, KY 40503
nasact.org

National Association of State
  Boards of Accountancy
150 Fourth Avenue N., Suite 700
Nashville, TN 37219
nasba.org

National Association of State
  Budget Officers
Hall of the States Building,
  Suite 642
444 North Capital Street NW
Washington, DC 20001
nasbo.org

National Association of Tax
   Professionals
720 Association Drive
P.O. Box 8002
Appleton, WI 54912
natptax.com

National Society of Accountants
1010 N. Fairfax Street
Alexandria, VA 22314
nsacct.org

Society of Financial Examiners
174 Grace Boulevard
Altamonte Springs, FL 32714
sofe.org

For information on educational institutions offering a specialization in accounting, contact:

Association to Advance Collegiate
   Schools of Business
777 S. Harbor Island Boulevard,
   Suite 750
Tampa, FL 33602
aacsb.org

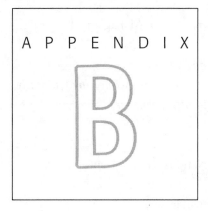

MAJOR ACCOUNTING JOURNALS OF ACADEMIC AND PROFESSIONAL SOCIETIES

The information in this appendix is listed alphabetically by society name. Each name is followed by the society's web address and the titles of the journals it publishes. Mailing addresses of the societies are listed in Appendix A. Many of the publications listed below are free to paid society members and available for a subscription fee to nonmembers. Some are delivered online only. In addition to these publications, many of the societies offer newsletters to members. Check the websites for complete information.

American Accounting Association
aaahq.org
The Accounting Review
Auditing: A Journal of Practice and Theory

American Taxation Association
aaahq.org
ATA Journal of Legal Tax Research
Journal of the American Taxation Association

American Institute of Certified Public Accountants
aicpa.org
Journal of Accountancy

American Society of Women Accountants
aswa.org
The Edge

Association of Government
   Accountants
agacgfm.org
*Government Financial
   Management TOPICS*
*The Journal of Government
   Financial Management*

Association to Advance Collegiate
   Schools of Business
aacsb.edu
BizEd Magazine

Information Systems Audit and
   Control Association
isaca.org
*Information Systems Control
   Journal*

Financial Executives International
fei.org
Financial Executive

Healthcare Financial Management
   Association
hfma.org
HFM Magazine

Institute of Internal Auditors
theiia.org
Internal Auditor

Institute of Management
   Accountants
imanet.org
Management Accounting Quarterly
Strategic Finance
Strategic TechNotes

National Association of Black
   Accountants
nabainc.org
Spectrum Magazine

National Association of Tax
   Professionals
natptax.com
TAXPRO Monthly
TAXPRO Quarterly Journal

National Society of Accountants
nsacct.org
NPA Magazine
NSA Technology Advisor

Society of Financial Examiners
sofe.org
Examiner

STATE BOARDS OF ACCOUNTANCY IN THE UNITED STATES

Alabama State Board of Public
Accountancy
P.O. Box 300375
Montgomery, AL 36130
asbpa.alabama.gov

Alaska State Board of Public
Accountancy
Department of Community and
Economic Development
Division of Occupational
Licensing
Box 110806
Juneau, AK 99811-0806
dced.state.ak.us/pcpa

Arizona State Board of
Accountancy
100 N. Fifteenth Avenue, Room
165
Phoenix, AZ 85007
accountancy.state.az.us

Arkansas State Board of
Accountancy
101 E. Capitol, Suite 430
Little Rock, AR 72201
state.ar.us/asbpa

California State Board of
Accountancy
2000 Evergreen Street, Suite 250
Sacramento, CA 95815-3832
dca.ca.gov/cba

Colorado State Board of
Accountancy
1560 Broadway, Suite 1370
Denver, CO 80202
dora.state.co.us/accountants

Connecticut State Board of
Accountancy
Secretary of the State
30 Trinity Street
P.O. Box 150470
Hartford, CT 06115
sots.state.ct.us/sboa/sboaindex.html

Delaware State Board of
Accountancy
Cannon Building, Suite 203
861 Silver Lake Boulevard
Dover, DE 19904
dpr.delaware.gov

District of Columbia Board of
Accountancy
941 North Capitol Street NE,
Room 7200
Washington, DC 20002
http://dcra.dc.gov

Florida Board of Accountancy
240 NW Seventy-sixth
Drive, A
Gainesville, FL 32607
myflorida.com

Georgia State Board of
Accountancy
237 Coliseum Drive
Macon, GA 31217
sos.state.ga.us/plb/accountancy/

Guam Board of Accountancy
335 S. Marine Corps Drive,
Suite 100
Tamuning, GU 96913
guamboa.org

Hawaii Board of Public
Accountancy
Department of Commerce and
Consumer Affairs
P.O. Box 3469
335 Merchant Street (96813)
Honolulu, HI 96801
hawaii.gov/dcca/areas/pvl/boards/
accountancy

Idaho State Board of Accountancy
P.O. Box 83720
Boise, ID 83720
state.id.us/boa

Illinois Board of Examiners
100 Trade Centre Drive
Champaign, IL 61820
ilboa.org

Illinois Department of Financial
and Professional Regulation
Public Accountancy Section
320 W. Washington Street, 3rd
Floor
Springfield, IL 62786
idfpr.com

Indiana Board of Accountancy
Indiana Professional Licensing
    Agency
Government Center South
402 W. Washington Street,
    Room W072
Indianapolis, IN 46204
state.in.gov/pla/bandc/accountancy

Iowa Accountancy Examining
    Board
1920 SE Hulsizer Avenue
Ankeny, IA 50021
state.ia/us/iacc

Kansas Board of Accountancy
Landon State Office Building
900 SW Jackson, Suite 556
Topeka, KS 66612
ksboa.org

Kentucky State Board of
    Accountancy
332 W. Broadway, Suite 310
Louisville, KY 40202
cpa.ky.gov

State Board of CPAs of Louisiana
601 Poydras Street, Suite 1770
New Orleans, LA 70139
cpaboard.state.la.us

Maine Board of Accountancy
Department of Professional and
    Financial Regulation
Office of Licensing and Regulation
35 State House Station
Augusta, ME 04333
maineprofessionalreg.org

Maryland State Board of Public
    Accountancy
500 N. Calvert Street, 3rd Floor
Baltimore, MD 21202
dllr.state.md.us/license/occprof/
    account.html

Massachusetts Board of Public
    Accountancy
239 Causeway Street, Suite 450
Boston, MA 02114
mass.gov/reg/boards/pa

Michigan Board of Accountancy
Department of Labor and
    Economic Growth
P.O. Box 30018
Lansing, MI 48909
michigan.gov/accountancy

Minnesota State Board of
    Accountancy
85 E. Seventh Place, Suite 125
St. Paul, MN 55101
boa.state.mn.us

Mississippi State Board of Public
    Accountancy
5 Old River Place, Suite 104
Jackson, MS 39202
msbpa.state.ms.us

Missouri State Board of
    Accountancy
P.O. Box 613
Jefferson City, MO 65102
http://pr.mo.gov/accountancy.asp

Montana State Board of Public
    Accountants
301 South Park
P.O. Box 200513
Helena, MT 59620
discovoeringmontana.com/dli/pac

Nebraska State Board of Public
    Accountancy
P.O. Box 94725
Lincoln, NE 68509
nol.org/home/bpa

Nevada State Board of
    Accountancy
1325 Airmotive Way, Suite 220
Reno, NV 89502
nvaccountancy.com

New Hampshire Board of
    Accountancy
78 Regional Drive, Building 2
Concord, NH 03301
state.nh.us/accountancy

New Jersey State Board of
    Accountancy
124 Halsey Street, 6th Floor
P.O. Box 45000
Newark, NJ 07101
state.nj.us/lps/ca/nonmed.htm

New Mexico Public Accountancy
    Board
5200 Oakland NE, Suite D
Albuquerque, NM 87113
rld.state.nm.us/b&c/accountancy/
    index.htm

New York State Board for Public
    Accountancy
State Education Department
Division of Professional Licensing
    Services
89 Washington Avenue, 2nd Floor
    East
Albany, NY 12234
op.nysed.gov/cpa.htm

North Carolina State Board of
    CPA Examiners
1101 Oberlin Road, Suite 104
P.O. Box 12827
Raleigh, NC 27605-2827
cpaboard.state.nc.us

North Dakota State Board of
    Accountancy
2701 S. Columbia Road
Grand Forks, ND 58201
state.nd.us/ndsba

Accountancy Board of Ohio
77 S. High Street, 18th Floor
Columbus, OH 43215
acc.ohio.gov

Oklahoma Accountancy Board
4545 Lincoln Boulevard, Suite 165
Oklahoma City, OK 73105
oab.state.ok.us

Oregon State Board of
  Accountancy
3218 Pringle Road SE, #110
Salem, OR 97302
http://egov.oregon.gov/boa

Pennsylvania State Board of
  Accountancy
2601 N. Third Street
Harrisburg, PA 17111
dos.state.pa.us/account

Puerto Rico Board of Accountancy
Box 9023271
Old San Juan Station
San Juan, PR 00902
estado.gobierno.pr/contador.htm

Rhode Island Board of
  Accountancy
233 Richmond Street, Suite 236
Providence, RI 02903
dbr.state.ri.us

South Carolina Board of
  Accountancy
110 Centerview Drive, Kingstree
  Building
P.O. Box 11329
Columbia, SC 29211-1329
llr.state.sc.us/pol/accountancy

South Dakota Board of
  Accountancy
301 E. Fourteenth Street, Suite 200
Sioux Falls, SD 57104
state.sd.us/dcr/accountancy

Tennessee State Board of
  Accountancy
500 James Robertson Parkway, 2nd
  Floor
Nashville, TN 37243
state.tn.us/commerce/boards/
  tnsba/index.html

Texas State Board of Public
  Accountancy
333 Guadalupe
Tower III, Suite 900
Austin, TX 78701
tsbpa.state.tx.us

Utah Board of Accountancy
P.O. Box 146741
Salt Lake City, UT 84114
dopl.utah.gov

Vermont Board of Public
    Accountancy
Office of Professional Regulation
26 Terrace Street, Drawer 09
Montpelier, VT 05609
vtprofessionals.org/opr1/
    accountants

Virginia Board of Accountancy
3600 W. Broadway Street,
    Suite 378
Richmond, VA 23230
boa.virginia.gov

Virgin Islands Board of Public
    Accountancy
Department of Licensing and
    Consumer Affairs
Office of Boards and Commissions
Golden Rock Shopping Center
Christiansted, St. Croix, VI 00822
dlca.gov.vi

Washington State Board of
    Accountancy
P.O. Box 9131
Olympia, WA 98507
cpaboard.wa.gov

West Virginia Board of
    Accountancy
122 Capitol Street, Suite 100
Charleston, WV 25301
wvboacc.org

Wisconsin Accounting Examining
    Board
1400 E. Washington Avenue
P.O. Box 8935
Madison, WI 53708
http://drl.wi.gov/index.htm

Wyoming Board of Certified
    Public Accountants
2020 Carey Avenue
Cheyenne, WY 82002
cpaboard.state.wy.us

APPENDIX

D

CANADIAN RESOURCES

CANADIAN INSTITUTE OF CHARTERED ACCOUNTANTS OFFICES

National Office

The Canadian Institute of
   Chartered Accountants
277 Wellington Street West
Toronto, ON M5V 3H2
cica.ca

ALBERTA, NORTHWEST TERRITORIES, AND NUNAVUT

The Institute of Chartered
   Accountants of Alberta
580 Manulife Place
10180–101 Street
Edmonton, AB T5J 4R2
icaa.ab.ca

BRITISH COLUMBIA AND YUKON TERRITORIES

The Institute of Chartered
   Accountants of British
   Columbia
505 Burrard Street, Box 22
Suite 500, One Bentall Centre
Vancouver, BC V7X 1M4
ica.bc.ca

MANITOBA

The Institute of Chartered
   Accountants of Manitoba
500–161 Portage Avenue East
Winnipeg, MB R3B 0Y4
icam.mb.ca

New Brunswick

The New Brunswick Institute of
Chartered Accountants
93 Prince William Street, 4th
Floor
Saint John, NB E2L 2B2
nbica.org

Newfoundland

The Institute of Chartered
Accountants of Newfoundland
95 Bonaventure Avenue, 5th Floor
P.O. Box 21130
St. John's, NF A1A 5B2
ican.nfld.ca

Nova Scotia

The Institute of Chartered
Accountants of Nova Scotia
1791 Barrington Street, Suite 1101
Halifax, NS B3J 3Z1
icans.ns.ca

Ontario

The Institute of Chartered
Accountants of Ontario
69 Bloor Street East
Toronto, ON M4W 1B3
icao.on.ca

Prince Edward Island

The Institute of Chartered
Accountants of Prince Edward
Island
P.O. Box 301
129 Kent Street, Suite 203
Charlottetown, PEI C1A 7K7
icapei.com

Québec

Ordre des Comptable Agréés du
Québec
680, rue Sherbrooke ouest,
18e étage
Montréal, QB H3A 2S3
ocaq.qc.ca

Saskatchewan

The Institute of Chartered
Accountants of Saskatchewan
1801 Hamilton Street, Suite 830
Regina, SK S4P 4B4
icas.sk.ca

CERTIFIED GENERAL ACCOUNTANTS ASSOCIATION OFFICES

National Office

800–1188 West Georgia Street
Vancouver, BC V6E 4A2
cga-online.org/canada

Alberta
900–926 Fifth Avenue SW
Calgary, AB T2P 0N7
cga-alberta.org

British Columbia
1867 West Broadway, 3rd Floor
Vancouver, BC V6J 5L4
cga-bc.org

Manitoba
4 Donald Street South
Winnipeg, MB R3L 2T7
cga-manitoba.org

**Student Services–Maritime
Region**
P.O. Box 5100
403–236 St. George Street
Moncton, NB E1C 8R2
cga-maritime.org

New Brunswick
10–236 St. George Street
Moncton, NB E1C 1W1
cga-nb.org

Newfoundland and Labrador
294 Freshwater Road, Suite 201
St. John's, NF A1B 1C1
cga-newfoundland.org

Northwest Territories/Nunavut
P.O. Box 128
5010 Fiftieth Avenue, 3rd Floor
Yellowknife, NT X1A 2N1
cga-nwt-nu.org

Nova Scotia
P.O. Box 73 CRO
Halifax, NS B3J 2L4
cga-ns.org

Ontario
240 Eglinton Avenue East
Toronto, ON M4P 1K8
cga-ontario.org

Prince Edward Island
P.O. Box 20151
Charlottetown, PEI C1A 9E3
cga-pei.org

Québec
445, Boulevard St. Laurent
Bureau 450
Montréal, QB H2Y 2Y7
cga-quebec.org

Saskatchewan
4–2345 Avenue C North
Saskatoon, SK S7L 5Z5
cga-saskatchewan.org

Yukon Territory

P.O. Box 31536
RPO, Main Street
Whitehorse, YT Y1A 6K8

International

Bahamas

P.O. Box N-7777
29 Retirement Road
3 Shirley Street
Nassau, Bahamas

Bermuda

Vallis Building, Ground Floor
46 Par-la-Ville Road
Hamilton, HM 11
Bermuda

Caribbean

CGA Student Services, Inc.
Suite 23, In One Accord Plaza
Warrens, St. Michael
Barbados

c/o IBT, Inc.
L'Anse Road, P.O. Box 1777
Castries, St. Lucia

c/o RBTT ROYTEC
136-138 Henry Street
Port of Spain, Trinidad

CERTIFIED MANAGEMENT ACCOUNTANTS OF CANADA OFFICES

National Office

CMA Canada
Mississauga Executive Centre
One Robert Speck Parkway, Suite 1400
Mississauga, ON L4Z 3M3
cma-canada.org

Alberta

Certified Management
    Accountants of Alberta
833 Fourth Avenue SW, Suite 1120
Calgary, AB T2P 3T5
cma-alberta.com

British Columbia

Certified Management
    Accountants of BC
P.O. Box 269
Two Bentall Centre, Suite 1055
555 Burrard Street
Vancouver, BC V7X 1M8
cmabc.com

Manitoba

CMA Canada—Manitoba Partner
815–240 Graham Avenue
Winnipeg, MB R3C 0J7
cma-canada.org/manitoba.asp

New Brunswick

Certified Management
   Accountants of New Brunswick
570 Queen Street, Suite 101
Fredericton, NB E3B 6Z6
cmanb.com/main

Newfoundland

Certified Management
   Accountants of Newfoundland
271 Thorburn Road
St. John's, NF A1B 4R1
cma-canada.org/newfoundland

Nova Scotia

Certified Management
   Accountants Nova Scotia and
   Bermuda
Senty Place
1559 Brunswick Street, Suite 500
Halifax, NS B3J 2G1
cmans.com

Northwest Territories

Certified Management
   Accountants of Northwest
   Territories
P.O. Box 512
Yellowknife, NT X1A 2N4
cma-canada.org/nwt

Ontario

Certified Management
   Accountants of Ontario
70 University Avenue, Suite 300
Toronto, ON M5J 2M4
cma-ontario.org

Québec

Certified Management
   Accountants of Québec
715, square Victoria
3 etage
Montréal, QB H2Y 2H7
cma-quebec.org

Saskatchewan

Certified Management
   Accountants of Sasketchewan
202–1900 Albert Street
Regina, SK S4P 4K8
cma-canada.org/saskatchewan

Yukon

Certified Management
   Accountants of Yukon
Territorial Representative
Yukon Territorial Government
Yukon YT Y1A 4N6
cma-canada.org.yukon

CANADIAN UNIVERSITIES OFFERING ACCOUNTING PROGRAMS

Alberta

Athabasca University
1 University Drive
Athabasca, AB T9S 3A3
athabascau.ca

University of Alberta
114 Street—89 Avenue
Edmonton, AB T6G 2M7
ualberta.ca

University of Calgary
2500 University Drive NW
Calgary, AB T2N 1N4
ucalgary.ca

University of Lethbridge
4401 University Drive
Lethbridge, AB T1K 3M4
uleth.ca

British Columbia

British Columbia Institute of
 Technology
3700 Willingdon Avenue
Burnaby, BC V53 VH2
ubc.ca

Kwantlen University College
 Surrey
12666 Seventy-Second Avenue
Surrey, BC V3W 2M8
kwantlen.bc.ca

Malaspina University College
900 Fifth Street
Nanaimo, BC V9R 5S5
mala.ca

Thompson Rivers University
Box 3010
900 McGill Road
Kamloops, BC V2C 5N3
tru.ca

University of British Columbia
2329 West Mall
Vancouver, BC V6T 1Z4
ubc.ca

University of Northern British
 Columbia
3333 University Way
Prince George, BC V2N 4Z9
unbc.ca

Manitoba

University of Manitoba
97 Dafoe Road
Winnipeg, MB R3T 2N2
umanitoba.ca

New Brunswick

Mount Allison University
Sackville, NB E4L 1E4
mta.ca

Newfoundland

Memorial University of
    Newfoundland
St. John's, NL A1C 5S7
mun.ca

Nova Scotia

Acadia University
Wolfville, NS B4P 2R6
acadiau.ca

Dalhousie University
Halifax, NS B3H 3J5
dal.ca

Mount Saint Vincent University
166 Bedford Highway
Halifax, NS B3M 2J6
msvu.ca

Saint Francis Xavier University
P.O. Box 5000
Antigonish, NS B2G 2W5
stfx.ca

Saint Mary's University
923 Robie Street
Halifax, NS B3H 3C3
stmarys.ca

University College of Cape Breton
P.O. Box 5300
Sydney, NS B1P 6L2
uccb.ns.ca

Ontario

Brock University
500 Glenridge Avenue
St. Catharine's, ON L2S 3A1
brocku.ca

Carleton University
1125 Colonel By Drive
Ottawa, ON K1S 5B6
carleton.ca

Lakehead University
955 Oliver Road
Thunder Bay, ON P7B 5E1
lakeheadu.ca

McMaster University
1280 Main Street West
Hamilton, ON L8S 4L8
mcmaster.ca

Queen's University
99 University Avenue
Kingston, ON K7L 3N6
queensu.ca

University of Toronto
Toronto, ON M5S 1A1
utoronto.ca

University of Waterloo
200 University Avenue West
Waterloo, ON N2L 3G1
uwaterloo.ca

University of Windsor
401 Sunset Avenue
Windsor, ON N9B 3P4
uwindsor.ca

Wilfrid Laurier University
75 University Avenue West
Waterloo, ON N2L C5
wlu.ca

York University
4700 Keele Street
150 Atkinson Building
Toronto, ON M3J 1P3
yorku.ca

Prince Edward Island

University of Prince Edward
   Island
550 University Avenue
Charlottetown, PEI C1A 4P3
upei.ca

Québec

Bishop's University
Lennoxville, QB J1M 1Z7
bishopsu.ca

Concordia University
1455 de Maisonneuve Boulevard
   West
Montréal, QB H3G 1M8
concordia.ca

McGill University
845 Sherbrooke Street West
Montréal, QB H3A 2T5
mcgill.ca

Universite Laval
Ste-Foy, QB G1K 7P4
ulaval.ca

Saskatchewan

University of Regina
3737 Wascana Parkway
Regina, SK S4S 0A2
uregina.ca

University of Saskatchewan
105 Administration Place
Saskatoon, SK S7N 5A2
usask.ca